Down In Wales

Visits to some wartime air crash sites

TERENCE R. HILL

GWASG Carreg Gwalch

ISBN: 0-86381-283-X

*Jacket Design by
Michael Hill*

*First published in 1994 by Gwasg Carreg Gwalch,
Iard yr Orsaf, Llanrwst, Gwynedd, Wales.*

☎ *0492 642031*

Printed and published in Wales.

Terence R. Hill

Son of an RAF Sergeant who took part in the Cape to Cairo flight of 1926, the Author was born in Ipswich, Suffolk in 1928. He joined the RAF in 1945 after hostilities had ended and unable to become aircrew, went into the motor transport branch working with many types of vehicle, in places as diverse as Scotland and Japan. In 1962, with the expansion of Transport Command, he was accepted as aircrew at the upper age limit. In the following twelve years he flew in many types of aircraft, taking part in relief operations in Nepal, evacuation of civilians from Cyprus during the emergency and experimental air dropping, in the course of which amassing nearly 5000 hours flying experience. He now lives in retirement near Aberystwyth.

Contents

Preface

As you wing your way to Spain, in the comparative luxury of a modern jet airliner, eating and drinking whilst flying at 500 mph, six miles up in the air, it is perhaps hard to understand why such large numbers of RAF and USAAF aircraft crashed in Wales and indeed all over the British Isles during the Second World War.

For the most part, enemy action had no part in these crashes; it was a combination of many factors. After aircrew had learnt the basic flying skills, they were sent to Operational Training Units where they were formed into crews and were taught to work as a team in using their aircraft, not simply as flying machines, but as weapons of war.

As the Bomber Command offensive against Germany gained momentum, so did the demand for more aircrew. More OTUs were set up, equipped in the main with older aircraft withdrawn from front line service, to cope with this demand. With the introduction of four-engined aircraft, Heavy Conversion Units supplemented the OTUs.

Most of the training was, of necessity, carried out away from Southern and Eastern England where operational flying was taking place, and a lot of this, especially from OTUs in the Midlands, took place over Wales.

Before the era of the jet engine, power was usually the limiting factor in an aircraft's load-carrying and performance capabilities and, as bomb loads increased, many aircraft were short of this essential commodity. Single-engined performance was marginal and in some cases, non-existent. Add to this, rudimentary de-icing equipment, most important when aircraft could not fly above the worst of the weather as they can today, very basic radio aids and a totally blacked-out countryside, then it can be seen that there was quite a hazardous combination. The often rainy, mist shrouded Welsh hills and mountains added one more most dangerous ingredient.

Although this book is mainly concerned with war-time crashes, two post-war jet fighter crashes have been included before the memories of those present grows dim with the passing of time, indeed one of those included was over 20 years ago. Aircraft malfunction and weather can still claim their victims.

During the 1939-1945 war, Bomber Command alone lost over 55,000 aircrew from Britain, the Commonwealth and our Allies; of those, over 5,000 died during training. It speaks volumes of these men when it is realised that RAF aircrew were then, as now, all volunteers.

It is to those men that this book is dedicated.

Introduction

Access to crash sites mentioned in this book is often across private land and the reader has no absolute right of entry, other than where there is a footpath or green road. Farmers are not keen on walkers wandering uninvited onto their land, particularly during lambing, and they should always be approached before proceeding. They will, almost without exception, be happy to admit you and direct you to the site. Many indeed, may well have lived there at the time of the crash and be very willing to tell you about it.

None of the sites described require any mountaineering skills. It should, however, be remembered that, what appears to be a nice spring day on lower ground may well turn out to be very cold at 2,000 feet; the drop in temperature due to altitude plus the wind-chill factor can often mean a difference of 10 degrees or more.

Many sites are also in areas of boggy land. It only takes one trip in high boggy country, like Pumlumon, when the cloud suddenly rolls in, enveloping one in a swirling, frightening fog, to realise that, although you may be only a few miles from civilisation, it feels like fifty!

You should take warm clothing, food, a map of course, wear good boots and carry a compass. If this last item seems a bit over the top for an ordinary walker, let me assure you that it is not. Should you get lost its use is obvious; many sites are however, difficult to pin-point without one. Weathered aircraft structure can look deceptively like rock and a compass can prevent you straying too far off course to investigate what may turn out to be wet, rock glinting in the sun.

It is best to travel with a companion, always let someone know where you are going and when you expect to return.

The map reference, using Ordnance Survey Landranger maps is given for each site and some are accompanied by a small diagram, but generally a detailed description of exactly how to get to the site is not given, allowing the reader to plan his or her own route.

Observe the Country Code and remember, even if you find nothing, the search will take you into some of the most beautiful countryside in Wales, well worth a visit on its own account.

T.R. Hill
1994

Identifying your Finds

After a time lapse of nearly 50 years, long gone are the days when almost complete aircraft could be found, especially on lower ground. The authorities have removed much debris; indeed in the Snowdonia National Park a lot has been taken away in a misguided attempt to "tidy" up the hills. The wreckage of all military aircraft in Britain belongs to the Ministry of Defence and should only be removed from the site with proper authorisation. If ammunition is found it should not be tampered with.

The main interest in finding any wreckage is not so that it can be recovered, but so that the searcher will know that he found the exact site, so leaving wreckage will help those that come along in years to come.

Of course, much of this debris will look rather like a lot of old scrap metal to the uninitiated, but on closer examination will often reveal inspector's stamps and manufacturer's marks which will help in identification.

The following is a list of identification marks to be found on aircraft mentioned in this book, although components made by subcontractors may not bear any of these marks.

Inspector's Stamps		Component Prefixes	
Armstrong-Whitworth	AW	P38 Lighting	22
Avro	R3	Wellington	284 & 285
De Havilland	DH	Mosquito	98
Fairey	F8/FY	Whitley	SP
Handley-Page	HP	Halifax	57
Republic	R	P47 Thunderbolt	89
Vickers-Armstrong	VA	Lancaster	683
Boulton and Paul	EP		

Part of rudder bar assembly;
Type 300 Spitfire

Wing structure P47
Thunderbolt

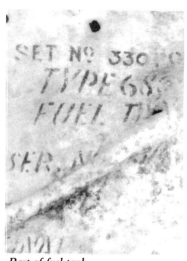

Part of fuel tank,
type 683 Lancaster

Aircraft Wreckage

The ownership of the remains of British, United States and German aircraft is vested in the Ministry of Defence.

Permission of that Ministry should be sought if it is intended to recover any parts found. This is mainly intended for groups who wish to actually excavate the site, and not really aimed at someone casually picking up a small item, however, technically, no part should be removed. This may seem a trifle ridiculous when it is known that groups, local councils, individuals etc., have been carting away wreckage wholesale for years. Really, it is best not to remove parts but to photograph them for later identification — this will also have the advantage of leaving something for successive generations to find.

The contact address for those who wish to recover items is:

Ministry of Defence, S 196 (Air)
Room 1074
Building 248
RAF INNSWORTH
GLOUCESTER GL3 1EZ

★ ★ ★

Maps

All references given in this book are for Ordnance Survey Landranger 1:50,000 series. 1¼ in. to the mile.

★ ★ ★

The Country Code

Respect the life and work of the countryside
Guard against all risk of fire
Leave gates as you find them
Keep dogs under control
Keep to public paths across farmland
Take your litter home
Protect wildlife, plants and trees
Take care on country roads
Help keep water clean
Don't damage trees, hedges and walls

Vickers-Armstrong's Wellington Mk 1C P9299

The Vickers-Armstrong's Wellington was the mainstay of Bomber Command during the early war years. After a disastrous start in daylight operations in 1939, it then operated at night with great success. Its "geodetic" construction, designed by Barnes Wallis, made it immensely strong and often aircraft returned from operations with great areas of their fabric covering missing. (Parts of this lattice work is usually evident at Wellington crash sites.) At one time there were 21 squadrons of Wellingtons, known affectionately as "Wimpeys", in Bomber Command, but by 1943 they were mostly replaced on operations by the newer four-engined bombers.

In 1941 Sgt Ward became the only member of a Wellington crew to be awarded the VC, when, on the return from a raid on Munster his aircraft was attacked over Holland by a BF110 night fighter. Sgt Ward climbed out of the astro-dome, and by kicking footholds in the fabric covering of the fuselage, made his perilous way to the starboard engine and put out the fire with a portable fire extinguisher. He was killed just two months later during an attack on Hamburg.

The Mark 1c was one of the most widely used variants of the Wellington, 2685 being built of the total of 11461 aircraft produced. It was powered by two Bristol Pegasus XVIII radial engines of 1000hp each, could attain a maximum speed of 235 mph, and carry a bomb load of 4500 lbs.

★ ★ ★

A Wellington prepares to take-off on a bombing raid. Note bomb bay doors still open.

Wellington N2980 at Brooklands Museum where it is being restored. The geodetic construction designed by Barnes Wallis is clearly shown.

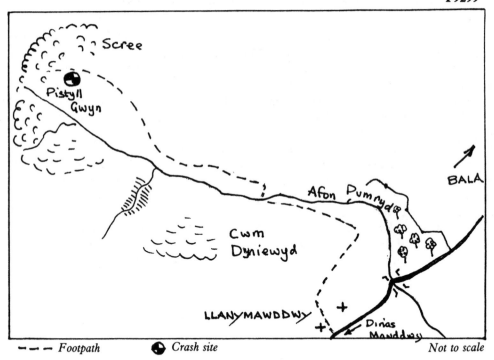

—··— *Footpath*   ⬤ *Crash site*   *Not to scale*

P9299, a Mark 1c, was delivered to the RAF in April 1940 and made its first operational flight on April 30th, when it took part in a raid on Stavanger aerodrome in Norway. During the next 14 months it took part in over 20 more attacks, including one when it had to crash land on return after being damaged during the raid. In June 1941 it was issued to the Czech Training Unit at East Wretham in Norfolk. Later renamed 1429 Flight it was really an offshoot of No. 311 (Czech) squadron and carried the same squadron code KX; P9299 being KX-A.

* * *

On April 6th 1942, Sgt Alois Keda and his trainee crew took off on a training exercise which was routed across North Wales. During the flight, the radio became unserviceable and when thick cloud was encountered the pilot decided to descend through it, no doubt thinking that they had reached the coast, in reality some 15 miles distant. He was, in fact, flying down Cwm Dyniewyd, a valley coming to a dead end at Pistyll Gwyn waterfall, near Llanymawddwy. The aircraft struck the hillside shortly after 1300 hrs and was totally destroyed. There were no survivors from the crew of six.

* * *

I was unable to find a map reference for the site; only a hiking book gave me any sort of clue. The site had, of course, been cleared some 40 years earlier and not knowing the exact spot had put me at a slight disadvantage to say the least. Firstly I looked at the waterfall. Doubtless an aircraft flying down the valley in bad visibility would go straight ahead hoping for a gap; but the rocks were steep, wet and slippery and I decided not to chance it.

I then looked over to the right where the steep slope was covered with loose scree; after all, a large aircraft does not crash on one little spot, it may well cover a large area. It also occurred to me, as an excuse to save me attempting the climb of the unstable surface, that, had an aircraft struck near the top, the wreckage would have fallen down the hillside. Even after the passage of many years, something could still be under the scree, perhaps even uncovered by the action of the weather and sheep moving about on it.

After about an hour, criss-crossing the scree slope I began to come across fragments; instrument parts, numerous unidentified pieces and a few pieces of geodetic framework, the fixing plates bearing the VA type no. 285 plus inspectors' stamps.

As I stood on the hillside I thought of that day, over 40 years previously, when on that very spot, 6 brave Czech airmen died.

MR 124/886196

A Wellington of No. 311 (Czech) Squadron

Fairey Battle K7589

The Fairey Battle entered service with the RAF in May 1937 and because production at the parent factory was supplemented by other firms in the expansion schemes immediately prior to the war, only a year or so later it equipped 15 squadrons. As with a number of aircraft of that period, although advanced at the time of its design, such was the pace of development that by the time it was used in action it was totally unsuitable for the task for which it was designed. The quoted top speed of 240 mph was rarely, if ever attainable and with a poor defensive armament, it proved easy prey for enemy fighters and ground fire alike.

In May 1940, during the German advance across the Low Countries, the Battle was flung into action in an attempt to stem the oncoming tide; its task was to destroy the river bridges at Maastricht and Sedan. In these operations, the Battle proved once and for all, its inadequacy, whereas its crews showed bravery unsurpassed in the short history of the RAF. At Maastricht, Fg. Off. Garland and Sgt Gray won the RAF's first VCs of the 1939-1945 war at the cost of their lives, and at Sedan 40 of the attacking force of 71 aircraft were lost.

Over 3,000 Battles were built, but after the Battle of France they were soon relegated to the training role where their pleasant handling characteristics proved an advantage.

* * *

In October 1938, however, the Battle was still in its heyday. 226 squadron was temporarily at Harwell, Berkshire at the time. On the 6th of the month, P. Off. A.L. McEwan, a Canadian, with Cpl. James and A.C. Clarke as crew members were briefed for a cross-country exercise incorporating some photography, to Ynys Enlli (*Bardsey Island*) off the Llŷn Peninsula, North Wales. By the time they had reached mid-Wales they had strayed, whether or not intentionally is not known, from the planned route and, whilst flying over unbroken low cloud and mist the pilot decided to descend through it, doubtless trying to fix his position. It must be remembered that there was no navigator as such on board and it was the pilot who was responsible for navigation.

The aircraft struck the hillside near Cwmbiga, on the eastern slopes of Pumlumon; all the crew members were killed.

A report in the *Western Mail* the next day stated that Mr Williams, a surveyor with the Forestry Commission, had seen the aircraft flying quite normally a few minutes before the crash, a statement rather at odds with the descent through the clouds. Minutes later he heard an explosion and rushed to the scene with all the men he could muster from the plantation, but the crew were beyond all aid.

David Lloyd, a shepherd, also heard the crash and saw a pall of smoke on the hillside and hurried as best he could the two miles or so to the spot, to find that the bodies of the crew were badly mutilated and charred almost beyond recognition. It took several hours for the bodies to be brought down the trackless mountainside.

* * *

When looking into the crash of Wellington PG312 (page 78), at Old Hall, I spoke to Mrs Jane Evans who lived there in 1938 and indeed still does, though in a different house. In addition to the Wellington, she told me about the Battle. Her brother-in-law and husband, now both deceased, had gone up to the scene in 1938 and she showed me photographs taken at the time. These were of great help to me as, up to that time I had been making a vain search for the site on level ground, whereas the photographs showed it to be on a steepish slope.

On course, there were other factors which had made previous searches difficult. The wrong map reference didn't help, but the major difficulty was, and still is, that a forest, the Hafren, has been planted over the whole area. Although the Forestry Commission allows members of the public to wander around, it still presents a rather daunting task. My first two visits proved fruitless, but my third, armed with a new map reference, proved successful. Harassed by clouds of small biting flies in the hot airless woods I had,

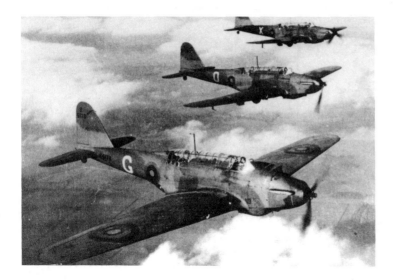

*Fairey Battles of
226 Squadron, 1939*

*In the immediate pre-war era,
aircraft carried the squadron number
on the side of the fuselage*

*Glyn Evans at the site of the
crash in 1938*

*Here, he inspects the Rolls-Royce
Merlin engine*

Three Die in R.A.F. Plane Crash on Welsh Mountain

SHEPHERD FINDS BODIES AFTER EXPLOSION

FORESTRY WORKERS DASH TO DESOLATE SPOT

THREE men attached to the R.A.F. station at Harwell, Didcot (Berkshire), lost their lives when their machine crashed into the mountain-side two miles from the summit of the Plinlimmon Range near Llanidloes, Montgomeryshire, yesterday.

The following communiqué was issued by the Air Ministry last night:—

"The Air Ministry regret to announce that Pilot-officer A. L. McEwan, Corpl. F. James, and Aircraftman Clark lost their lives in an accident at Plinlimmon (Montgomeryshire) to-day to an aircraft of No. 220 ("B") Squadron Harwell.

"Pilot-officer McEwan was the pilot and Corpl. James and Aircraftman Clark the only other members of the crew."

The machine appeared to have been blown to pieces by an explosion.

No one actually saw the disaster happen, but Mr. David Lloyd, a shepherd, was in his house when he heard a loud explosion.

On going outside he saw smoke on the hill about two miles away. He hastened to the spot and found the remnants of the aeroplane.

He came across one man who was badly mutilated, and further on he encountered two more bodies. All the men were dead.

Apparently Normal

Mr. Humphrey Williams, a surveyor employed by the Forestry Commission, had seen the aeroplane a few minutes before the crash flying apparently normally.

Within two minutes he heard an explosion. He (in) two then came considerable distance away, but immediately proceeded to the scene of the crash with all ...

Two-mile Trek

The foresters had a two-mile trek across rough mountainous country to the wrecked machine.

The charred bodies of the men, which were almost unidentifiable, were examined by Dr. Graham Davies.

It took several hours to bring the bodies over the trackless mountain-side, the spot where the tragedy occurred being a mile and a half from the nearest farmhouse.

Plinlimmon is the centre of a great mountain group containing the sources of the Severn, Wye, and three other Welsh rivers. It is 2,468ft. high and lies on the borders of Cardiganshire and Montgomeryshire, 12 miles west of Llanidloes.

many men as he could gather from the plantation.

He saw that the airmen were beyond all aid and sent for the police. They arrived later and the bodies were taken to the mortuary at Llanidloes.

BOMBER WITH CREW OF 5 MISSING

ANGLO-ITALIAN RELATIONS

LORD PERTH SEES CIANO AGAIN

Fresh Instructions From London

ROME, Thursday.

Acting on fresh instructions from London, Lord Perth had a further conversation with Count Ciano, the Italian Foreign Minister, to-day. The interview was the fourth on successive days.

It is understood that the instructions contained no concrete proposals, but ...

Troops P...

JERUSA...

...were rather in the nature of a series of observations by the British Government on the problem of Anglo-Italian relations and the Spanish war.

FASCIST GRAND COUNCIL

ROME, Thursday.

The Fascist Grand Council met to-night and among the subjects believed to have been discussed were Italy's relations with Britain and France and their bearing on the Spanish situation.—Reuter.

Western Mail October 1938

CRASH SITE

FOREST TRACKS

Western edge of forest

HAFREN FOREST

Staylittle

Fallen trees

CWMBIGA

Fuches

Unfenced road

In the Hafren: the part of K7589 can be seen on the right

Part of cockpit canopy. Brush marks in paint can be seen around screw heads

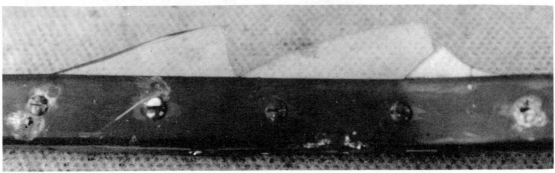

14

after nearly two hours of searching, just about reached the end of my tether, when I came across a tree blown over by the previous years' gales. There, in its roots, was a small hinged panel; a wipe over revealed original green interior paint, a Fairey inspection stamp and serial number.

The trouble with mature forest sites is that the roots of adjoining rows of trees seem to intertwine, forming an impenetrable suspended floor, covering everything underneath. Occasionally there is a gap and, just under the surface at one such gap, I came across my most exciting find — a piece of cockpit canopy frame about a foot long, with fragments of Perspex still attached and with the original dark earth external paintwork in good condition. Indeed, the matt paint had been touched up by hand, the original brush marks clearly visible as they skipped over small areas behind the raised screw heads! What a lot has happened in the world since the ground crew at Harwell, or Usworth the Battles' main base, took the paint pot out to K7589 in 1938.

A visit to the RAF Museum showed this fragment to be part of the forward sliding canopy frame (I always photograph my finds now to assist in later recognition).

When the trees in this part of the forest are felled, harvesting is a continuous process, much more will probably come to light.

MR 136/839893

Battle Postscript

In December 1993 I decided to re-visit the site. On arriving at the nearest point on the track to the crash location I discovered that a swathe of trees about 200 yards deep had been felled; the site was therefore only about another 100 yards into the forest, but the different tree line, plus the fact that more trees had been blown down in gales, made finding the original location almost impossible. Again, by sheer luck, after 1½ hours fruitless search, I came upon the complete port undercarriage oleo embedded in the roots of a tree. The identification plate showed that it had been manufactured on February 24th 1938. The aircraft was therefore in service for 8 months at the most before the crash, and, 55 years later, was chanced upon in a forest in the foothills of Pumlumon.

A word of warning. Where trees have been felled in the forest, much debris remains, including small trees. They soon become covered in moss and bracken so walking over the area is extremely hazardous.

*Port undercarriage leg discovered in
Hafren Forest 55 years after crash*

Bristol Blenheim Mk IV L9039

The Bristol Blenheim was a twin-engined light bomber and fighter aircraft. It was powered by two Bristol "Mercury" radial engines, developing 920 hp each, and in its Mark IV version had a top speed of 266 mph.

It first came into service with the RAF in 1937 and created something of a sensation in that it outpaced the biplane fighters in service at the time. However, by the outbreak of war in 1939, the biplane fighters had been largely superceded by much faster monoplanes, such as the Spitfire and the Hurricane and on the German side by the Bf. 109. The comparatively low speed and poor armament of the Blenheim made it very vulnerable from the air and especially to groundfire. Nevertheless, Blenheim crews showed outstanding courage in pressing home their attacks against heavily defended targets; from September 4th, 1939, when German shipping was attacked with the loss of 5 aircraft, (107 Squadron lost 4 of the 5 Blenheims despatched) to August 17th, 1942, when 18 Squadron attacked airfields in the Holland, the last Bomber Command Blenheim operation.

Wg. Cdr. Edwards was awarded the VC during a daylight raid by 105 Squadron on Bremen in July 1941.

* * *

On April 9th, 1940, Blenheim L9039, coded LD-Y of No. 13 OTU Bicester, Oxfordshire, took-off on a night cross-country flight in company with another Blenheim, to the Isle of Man. Sgt A. Hall was at the controls, with Sgts Graham and Cotton and LAC James as the other crew members. Encountering low cloud over Llangollen, the other aircraft climbed to 4,500 feet, but Sgt Hall obviously not aware of his position, continued on at low level striking the high cliffs of Craig-yr-Ysfa killing all those on board. This was one of the earliest war-time crashes in the area. The aircraft struck the rock face near the top of the ridge and the wreckage fell down the slope; the fuselage, long since disappeared, was shown in early photographs, lodged high up in a gully.

There must have been explosion on impact, as many parts were found, a fuel tank amongst them, many hundreds of yards away. After 50 years, however, very little wreckage, other than very heavy items is now in its original position.

* * *

An easy walk along the flat valley floor, past a reservoir and old mine workings, all the time moving further towards a great semi-circle of high cliffs rising to over 2,000 feet. Over to the right, the often snow-covered peak of Carnedd Llewelyn.

The path turns away to the North, but a compass check shows the site to be to the West. The way is barred by boggy ground and a detour is made nearer the base of the cliffs.

Much wreckage remains, including the two "Mercury" engines, although some cylinders are missing. Many fragments and much metal skinning lie about.

This is a marvellous walk; constantly looking over one's shoulder on the return journey just to look at the scenery. An easy 3 hours.

MR 115/694638

Bristol Blenheim Mk. IV

*The massive face of
Craig-yr-Ysfa*

*One engine lies amongst the rocks
of Craig-yr-Ysfa. The aircraft
crashed at the top right hand corner
of the picture.*

*Engine cylinder showing
valves and springs.*

Avro Anson AX583

The Avro Anson was a twin-engined aircraft which, although operational during the early war years in Coastal Command, spent the remainder of the war as a navigational, wireless and gunnery training aircraft. It was powered by two Armstrong-Siddeley Cheetah radial engines of 420 hp each and had a maximum speed of 188 mph. In September 1939 the first attack on a German U-boat was made by an Anson of 500 Sqn. Nearly 7000 Ansons were built in Britain and many were built in Canada.

No. 2 Observer's Advanced Flying Unit was one of a number of units based in N. England and Wales where navigators received their training. With trainee crews and aircraft of rather limited performance it is not really surprising that the wreckage of perhaps 30 Ansons litter the mountains and hills of Wales.

On April 25th 1944, Anson AX 583 took off from No. 2 OAFU Millom on the Cumbrian coast with Sgt R. Smith as pilot and P. Off. Polomark (RCAF) as navigator, on a night exercise over North Wales. They crossed the coast near Conwy at 2000 feet but nearly 5 degrees off course. The aircraft hit the eastern side of Drum in the Carneddau range. All five crew members were killed.

* * *

The site is reached after a long trudge through lumpy, soggy, heather-covered moorland, with water-filled, almost invisible holes to trap the unwary foot. The cloud on this day is thick, low and fast moving. Occasionally it breaks to reveal captivating views of the Conwy valley, the odd shaft of sunlight sparkling on the river. To the north-east the Great Orme can be glimpsed, whilst over to the north, the sea is bright blue with a tiny sailing boat making its way past Penmaenmawr. The cloud thickens again, swirling around the moor, cutting one off in a lonely, almost frightening world. Through a break, a USAF F111 roars past, just managing to keep in visual contact with the ground. Heather no longer grows on the main point of impact, a black, peaty area strewn with much small wreckage. It is first spotted, however, because the undercarriage framework, complete with some gears, stands up above the heather. Because of the sturdy construction, undercarriage parts often remain, but because of steel parts used in them, are usually badly corroded.

The Anson had a large amount of wood in its construction, some marks having wooden wings, AX 583 being one of these, and the site is littered with brass wood screws, an unusual sight for those more used to all-metal aircraft. Metal skinning and panels are there in profusion, some still having the bright yellow paint still in evidence.

A sad reminder of the tragedy was the discovery of a metal battledress or trouser button of the type used on war-time uniforms.

MR 115/715698

The crash site overlooking Conwy valley.

Vickers-Armstrong's Wellington Mk 1C R1068

At 1100 hours on August 17th 1941 Sgt James Stuart, a pilot on 'A' Flight 21 OTU Moreton-in-the-Marsh, Gloucestershire, took off with a trainee crew on a cross-country flight over Wales in Wellington R1068.

Some 30 minutes later, whilst flying above cloud, what appeared to be the coastline was glimpsed and the aircraft began a descent through the cloud. All crews had been warned not long before to allow a 10 minute margin after their ETA at the coast before descending. The apparent coastline was, however, the northern bank of the Dyfi estuary and the aircraft struck the mountainside at Rhosfarch above Pennal. There is a memorial to the crew at Pennal on the wall of the cemetery.

★ ★ ★

The site, like many others after a period of 50 years, has been looked at many times, recently with no success whatsoever, but I made enquiries at Rhosfarch farm after hearing stories locally of sharp bangs being heard on the hillside when the farmer decided to use a harrow on the ground in order to improve the grass for the sheep. These "bangs" were exploding 0.33″ ammunition!

21 OTU Moreton-in-the-Marsh 1944. A line-up of Vickers-Armstrong's Wellingtons.

R1068 crash site with River Dovey in background.

19

*Frazer-Nash gun turret in
Brooklands Museum together with
fragment found at Rhosfarch.*

*Memorial to crew in wall
of Pennal Cemetery.*

One and a half hours searching the hillside revealed quite an amount of small wreckage, mainly airframe fragments and exploded cartridge cases. Two interesting parts did come to light; one a piece of alloy channel framework painted dark green and having a distinctive little bracket with a small hole drilled through it. I despaired of discovering exactly what it was, until I was invited to Brooklands Museum to inspect the Wellington fuselage which is being restored, and discovered the piece to be part of the framework of the Frazer-Nash gun turret. The other part was soon recognised; it was the end of the rudder bar assembly. One piece that I found proved very interesting but I could not for the life of me recognise it. I took it to the Brooklands Museum but even the experts there were just as baffled. One thing was certain, it had an Air Ministry reference number on it, 5A/1151; this proved that it was not part of the aircraft structure but something that could be carried in various aircraft, probably of an electrical nature. Imagine my surprise, therefore, when visiting an aerojumble at Tangmere Aviation Museum, to discover a new one on a stall loaded with war surplus odds and ends. It turns out to be the glass lens used in an Aldis lamp, a device used for sending messages, or with different coloured glasses, flashing the colours of the day etc.

MR 135/688025

*End of rudder bar assembly of R1068
found on site.*

Boeing B17G Flying Fortress 44-6005

The first American Army Air Force bombers began to arrive in Britain in July 1942, first in a trickle and then an ever-growing force that was eventually larger than RAF Bomber Command. The Eighth Air Force, as it was known, was equipped with two types of four engined heavy bomber, the Consolidated B24 Liberator and the Boeing B17 Flying Fortress. With the RAF by night and the USAAF by day the 3rd Reich was subjected to the heaviest aerial bombardment hitherto not seen in the war.

The spearhead of the daylight attack was the B17 Flying Fortress, a four engined aircraft with a speed of 280 mph and thirteen 0.5″ guns to defend itself, but compared with the Lancaster, quite a small bomb load. To compensate for this, operating in daylight meant that greater accuracy could be achieved. Of the total of 12761 B17's produced during the war 8680 were of the 'G' variant. 44-6005 was built by the Douglas Aircraft Corporation of Santa Monica California and belonged to the 351st Bomb Group at Polebrook, the very field where the first B17 landed on July 6th 1942.

On June 8th, 1945 44-6005 left Polebrook, with Lt Johnson as pilot, with 19 on board, on the first leg of the journey that was to take them back to the USA. On approaching Valley in Anglesey, their first stop, the pilot asked for a course to steer as thick cloud covered the ground and made a visual approach impossible. For some unknown reason, he did not take this course, but, crossing the coast south of Barmouth in low cloud and mist, struck Craig-cwm-llwyd, with the loss of all on board. Farmers and shepherds were reported in the *Western Mail* as having heard the aircraft above the clouds. The wreckage and the trail it made as it slid down the mountain could be seen from Barmouth.

* * *

A war-weary Boeing B17G Flying Fortress.

I had visited the area twice, in an attempt to locate the site, with no success, but decided to make a final effort. I was lucky to come across an elderly farmer and his assistant shearing sheep, who told me that he had been in the field lower down the hillside at the time of the crash. He said that there were many bright fires and a large item, which he took to be a wheel, rolled down the hillside, smashing through a dry-stone wall before coming to rest. He pointed out to me the dark patch on the hillside where the aircraft had crashed.

I soon found where the dry-stone wall had been repaired (it was in fact an engine which had rolled down the hillside) and a short search produced a fragment of alloy. At the main impact point I found masses of unidentifiable pieces of metal, but also a gold fountain pen knib, hydraulic pipe unions, parachute fabric and assorted fuses. The reason for the bright fires turned out to be pools of melting magnesium.

The farmer told me that there had been talk at the time of the compasses being affected by the rocks, causing the aircraft to take up a reciprocal heading, but the real cause will probably never be known.

Now all that remains is a dark patch of earth to mark the spot where 19 men, whose war was over, died before reaching home.

MR 124/645122

The remains of 44-6005 lie in the foreground on Craig-cwm-llwyd. The sea and the Mawddach estuary are at the top of the picture.

Handley-Page Halifax B Mk 11 HR723

During the war, it was the policy of the Air Ministry to order two or three types of aircraft to each specification, mainly in order to guard against failure of an individual design. This policy extended right up to the "V" bomber era, with the Valiant, Vulcan and Victor all seeing service concurrently.

In the event, although the aircraft entered service at different times, it did mean that many squadrons operated aircraft that were not really the best available at the time; it would have disrupted production too much to abandon the less satisfactory types to concentrate on the best.

The Handley-Page Halifax was the first four engined bomber to drop bombs on Germany, but although 6,176 Halifaxes were built and it took part in most of Bomber Command's important attacks, it always seemed to be overshadowed by the Lancaster. Whereas the Lancaster operated throughout the war with basically the same mark, the Halifax needed many modifications before it eventually realised its full potential. One of the faults of the Halifax seems to have been difficulty in controlling the aircraft under certain conditions, resulting in the aircraft getting into an uncontrollable spin. A famous bomber pilot in his memoirs* mentions the concern caused by this characteristic. R.A. Read, who completed a tour of operations on Mark II Halifaxes, later becoming a flight commander instructor at 1666 HCU, told me that the cause of many Halifax crashes was a rudder overbalance which, in violent evasive action, caused the aircraft to go into a spiral dive usually with catastrophic results. Safety was not helped by an overcomplicated fuel system, which even in the Pilot's notes seemed "totally mystifying".

An assessment of the earlier marks of Halifax is best given in Ron Read's own words " . . . both Merlin engined versions were bloody awful aeroplanes and the Halifax only became alive with the introduction of the Mark III version with Bristol Hercules engines." (It is ironic that when Hercules engines were fitted to the Lancaster it too became a far superior aircraft. However, only 302 of this type were built as these engines were needed to make the Halifaxes' performance acceptable.)

★ ★ ★

At 1925 hours on October 27th 1944, Halifax HR723 OF 1666 HCU took-off from Wombleton near Helmsley, Yorkshire, on a cross-country training flight, with Flt Lt M.A. O'Neill (RCAF) at the controls. The aircract was flying below briefed height near the North Wales coast, possibly to identify landmarks, and in so doing began to pick up ice.

At this juncture the pilot should have used higher engine r.p.m. and warm air heating, but the ice was already building up, causing loss of power, probably by obstructing the carburettor air intakes, so that the aircraft could not be controlled satisfactorily.

The Captain ordered the crew to bale out and, with the exception of the wireless operator, they did so successfully sustaining only minor injuries. The W/op in his hurry to leave the darkened aircraft failed to notice the leg-straps of his parachute dangling beneath him. When he jumped there was nothing to support his body and he fell from the harness to his death. The aircraft crashed into a small field at Pydew, near Llandudno Junction, at 2330 hours, and burnt out.

The official report of the accident blames the pilot for aircraft mis-handling and poor airmanship.

★ ★ ★

With no map reference, I decided to make enquiries, calling at a number of houses, eventually arriving at the house of Mrs Hannah Jones who told me the whole story.

It was 11.00 pm, all was still; suddenly, their landgirl who lodged nearby, banged on the door in an agitated state and announced that an aeroplane had crashed on Bodysgawen.

Mrs Jones ran to the house next door (the one she lives in now) where an old couple were sitting before the fire, completely unconcerned, having heard nothing. She then ran to the crash to check that her father's calves grazing there, were safe. She found that they had managed to run away unharmed.

* The Everlasting Arms: John Searby

HR723, a Handley-Page Halifax B Mark 2 series 1A (special) seen here in 1943 in the markings of 405 Pathfinder squadron, where it took part in 3 of the attacks during the Battle of Hamburg. It flew with two other squadrons before being allocated to 1666 HCU. This is the actual aircraft which crashed at Pydew.

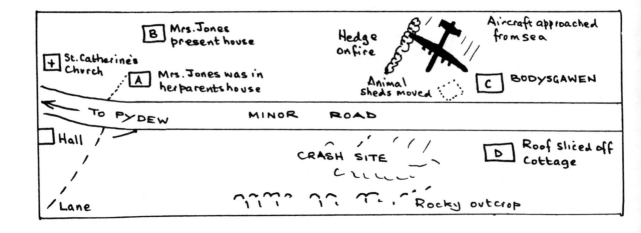

St. Catherine's Church

B — Mrs. Jones present house

A — Mrs. Jones was in her parents house

Hedge on fire

Aircraft approached from sea

Animal sheds moved

C — BODYSGAWEN

TO PYDEW — MINOR ROAD

Hall

CRASH SITE

D — Roof sliced off Cottage

Lane

Rocky outcrop

Bodysgawen, now known by a different name. Sheep now graze where the aircraft burned.

Further investigation revealed that the animal sheds adjoining Bodysgawen cottage had been completely detached from it and pushed forward, towards the road. A sow lay dead and her piglets ran loose. The old, solidly built cottage itself stood firm, the occupants miraculously unharmed, whilst the nearby hedge blazed in a spectacular fashion, and a horse was singed. The roof of the cottage across the road was smashed away but again, with great good fortune no one was hurt. The remains of the aircraft smouldered in the field; an engine was found up the footpath and wreckage was scattered everywhere.

Later, I met Mrs Jones' son who told me that when rebuilding the cottage many years ago he had cleared up a large amount of wreckage and buried it and a lot of builders' rubble in the field. It included four engine cylinders (unlikely, this was an in-line engined machine), but he could not remember exactly where it was buried, and in any case, it would take a JCB to get it out, and that would not really tell us any more than was known already. However, he gave me permission to look over the field in case any odd items remain. I found a number of pieces of engine casting and lots of unidentified fragments. One piece I photographed for later reference, was a section of fibrous material with a 10B serial number which has defied all attempts to identify it, despite the efforts of RAF storekeepers. It is probably connected with radio or radar equipment.

MR116/813793

Junkers Ju 88 A6 Werke No. 3459 5K + DW

The Junkers Ju 88 twin-engined bomber was perhaps the most effective of all German bombers in World War II. Powered by two Junkers "JUMO" 211J engines of 1340 hp each it was capable of a speed of 270 mph. It was armed with nine 7.9mm machine guns and could carry a bomb load of some 3300 lbs.

★ ★ ★

On April 25th, 1942, Fg. Off. Wyrill, a pilot with 225 squadron RAF, attended a briefing with his navigator F. Sgt Willins. No. 225, a night fighter squadron with the rather apposite motto "AD AURORAM" meaning "To the break of dawn", was based at High Ercall in Shropshire. The purpose of their flight later that night, was to carry out radar practice in conjunction with Honiley G.C.I. (Ground Controlled Interception) station. Their Beaufighter NF Mk. 6 had only just entered service and this would be a good opportunity to assess its capabilities, (or rather perhaps, the capabilities of the improved radar it carried).

Meanwhile, some hundreds of miles away at Evere, Brussells, Oberleutnant Gunter Brixius of IV Kampfgeschwader 3, also attended a briefing with his crew, comprising Oberfeldwebel Walter Kreienbrock (bomb aimer/gunner), Oberfeldwebel Paul Kocham, (Radio Operator) and Feldwebel Adolf Liedig (gunner). They were to take part in an attack on the cathedral city of Bath, in reprisal for RAF attacks on Germany. These raids were not aimed at military installations at all and were nicknamed "Baedeker Raids", as it was widely believed that the targets were just taken, more or less haphazardly, from the well-known travel guides of that name. Gunter Brixius' part in this operation was, using Ju 88 5K + DW, to make attacks on RAF night fighter bases that would be attempting to intercept the main force. Shortly after crossing the English coast, however, the RDF (radio direction finding) equipment developed a fault and he was soon completely lost. The bomb load was jettisoned and, doubtless, at this time, the crew were frantically looking for some sort of landmark to fix their position. Over blacked-out enemy countryside, this was not easy.

Whilst Ob. Lt Brixius and his crew were thus engaged, Fg. Off. Wyrill and F. Sgt Willins had taken off from High Ercall in Beaufighter X7933 and were carrying out their Radar training. Soon, however, ground control reported an unidentified aircraft a few miles from their position.

There then began a game of cat and mouse, during which both aircraft were reported to have come very close to the ground. Eventually Fg. Off. Wyrill★ got in a long burst of cannon fire, the enemy aircraft hit the ground on the lower slopes of Gwaunceste Hill, near Builth Wells and exploded in flames. Two of the crew managed to bale out and were captured but the pilot and gunner were killed. The bodies were taken down to a barn in Llanhailo farm and later buried in nearby Glascwm churchyard. In the 1960s their bodies were re-interred in the German War Cemetery at Cannock Chase, north of Birmingham. The wooden cross used over their grave is still inside Glascwm's peaceful country Church.

★ ★ ★

I decided to start my search at Llanhailo farm, and was lucky enough to meet the present farmer who allowed me to walk across the fields to the site, now covered by forestry. (There is an easier route using a footpath all the way, by going to the next farm up the road to the north east, about a mile distant). Despite the forestry, the site is easy to find, being only a few yards from the northern edge of the wood; debris is scattered amongst the trees. Although most of it is now very badly corroded, I managed to find part of the radiator or oil cooler matrix and a rusty fuel injector. Nearby, two pieces of crumbling aluminium have been wired together in the shape of a cross and there is a stake bearing a small engraved plate to the memory of Gunter Brixius and Adolf Liedig.

★ Fg. Off. Wyrill was killed later that year, during an enemy air-raid on Maison Blanche airfield, North Africa. He is buried in El Alia cemetery Algiers.

A Ju 88 in flight
(Bundesarchiv 363 2258m).

A Bristol Beaufighter in
night-fighter camouflage.

Left: The cross at Glascwm church
where they were buried. They were
later re-interred at the War Cemetery
at Cannock.

Above: The crash site, now covered
by trees showing the cross made from
the wreckage and next to it a plaque
in memory of the two German crew
members who were killed.

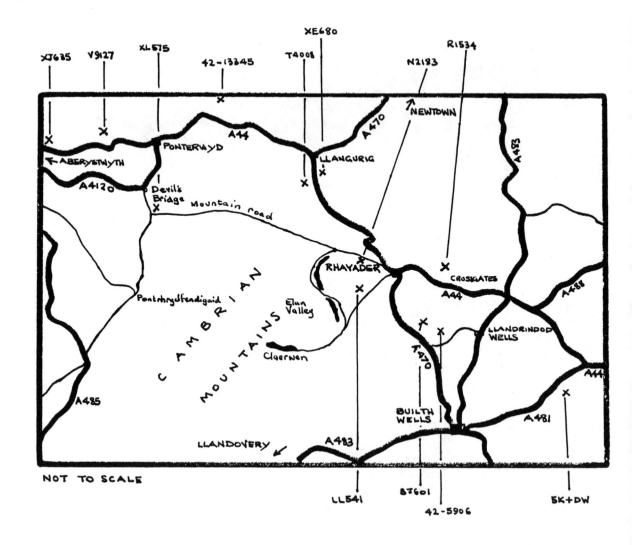

Twelve sites are in this small area
of mid-Wales.

Vickers-Armstrong's Wellington Mk 1C R1597

On April 8th, 1942, a Wellington bomber, R 1597, took off on a cross-country flight from 23 OTU Pershore piloted by Sgt R. Kennedy. A message was received at 14:35 hrs and at that time nothing appeared to be wrong, but one hour later the aircraft crashed in flames, near Troed-y-rhiw farm, at Llangamarch Wells. All seven on board were killed.

Although, in such cases, the cause of the accident is very difficult to find, it was deemed that the aircraft had flown into cumulo-nimbus cloud, (a particularly dangerous thunderstorm cloud, avoided even today, with the use of weather warning radar) and possibly been struck by lightning.

R1597 was delivered to the RAF on February 27th, 1941 and, whilst on operations with 218 Squadron, had been damaged. After repair it was delivered to 23 OTU in October 1941 and, after the crash, was recovered by no. 78 Maintenance Unit. It had flown a total of 318 hours.

★ ★ ★

As the present occupants of Troed-y-rhiw farm were comparative newcomers, I went to nearby Troed-y-rhiw Fach farm. Here I met Mr Price, who lived there at the time and was able to tell me all about the crash, although he says that there was no thunder at the time. Pointing out exactly where the aircraft had come down, only a few hundred yards up the hillside from the farm. He went across to see the wreckage on that fateful day but told me that he wished that he hadn't, because the human remains scattered around upset him.

After seeing the owners of Troed-y-rhiw, I had no difficulty in locating the spot, but little remains today; nothing on the surface and just a few fragments under the rock-hard ground.

This is a case of great interest, in that one can speak to people who were there at the time and locate the exact site where the disaster occurred; much more satisfying than just finding wreckage.

MR 147/955470

A Wellington from an OTU takes-off on a training flight.

The view standing on the crash site of R1597 at Troed-y-rhiw near Llangamarch Wells..

Handley-Page Hampden L4085

The Hampden, with the Whitley and Wellington formed the backbone of Bomber Command in the early war years and, like the Wellington, proved unable to defend itself successfully in daylight operations. Unlike the others, the Hampden had no power operated turrets, relying only on manually operated guns which had a limited field of fire. It had, however, a tidy turn of speed, was very manoeuverable and could carry 4,000 lb of bombs. Powered by two Bristol Pegasus radial engines, it could attain a speed of 250 mph and had a range of 1,200 miles.

Two VCs were awarded to Hampden crew members: the first to Flt Lt Learoyd and the second to an air gunner, Sgt J. Hannah who climbed outside the aircraft in flight to extinguish a fire.

★ ★ ★

On the night of July 31/August 1st, 1940, a force of 42 Hampdens, Battles and Blenheims took off to attack a variety of targets and to lay mines in enemy waters. An early victim of "friendly fire" was one of these Battles, shot down in error by RAF fighters.

On their return, most of Eastern England was shrouded by fog and three Hampdens were forced to ditch in the sea. L4085 was one of these.

Sgt Farmer was the pilot of L4085 of 44 Squadron Waddington and had taken part in the night's operations. Returning to foggy Lincolnshire he could find no way down through the murk and continued flying in a westerly direction, hoping for a break, but without success. It was only when the lights of the neutral Irish Republic came into view that Sgt Farmer, having no wish to be interned for the rest of the war, turned onto a reciprocal heading and continued eastwards towards the Welsh coast. At about 0600 hours, having airborne for nearly 6 hours and with the mountains of Wales in sight, the engines spluttered to a stop, the fuel tanks dry.

He put the aircraft down into a sea which was calm, with only a slight swell. The Hampden floated for a few minutes during which time the rear guns were fired in an attempt to attract the attention of those on shore. Meanwhile, the dinghy was inflated, only to burst at once! The lower gunner/Observer, Sgt Don Seager, held onto the remains of it to stay afloat. Two vessels were launched from Aberystwyth: *Frederick Angus*, the lifeboat, and *Emerald Star* a motor boat. They put to sea at 0726 hours and, after a lengthy search, did not return until after mid-day. The crew had become separated in the water and one man was drowned as he tried to swim to the shore. Sgt Hobbs (the navigator) and Sgt Seager were picked up by Aberystwyth lifeboat several hours later. The other member of the crew was also rescued but his injuries were severe and he died later.

Don Seager reported that the firing of L4085s guns had been heard on the shore and the alarm had been raised but there had been a delay in launching the lifeboat because the maroon could not be fired during war-time. A man had to be despatched on his bicycle to round up the lifeboatmen!

After a spell in hospital in Aberystwyth, Don Seager recovered from his ordeal and went on two weeks sick leave, which, in turn, led to a bitter twist to the story. When his leave ended, Don made his way to King's Cross station to catch the train back to Lincoln. The air-raid sirens sounded but Don rightly assumed that the docks would be the target for the enemy aircraft and continued to wait on the platform. The anti-aircraft batteries began banging away at the attackers and Fate, in the form of an anti-aircraft shell that had failed to explode in the air, arrived on the platform and exploded close to Don. It caused such severe injuries that he had to have one leg amputated.

★ ★ ★

As the aircraft crashed some three and a half miles WSW of Aberystwyth, this one site that will be out of the reader's grasp; even a sub-aqua enthusiast would find the area too large to search.

If you climb to the top of Pen Dinas, to the south of Aberystwyth, you will find a monument in the

A Handley-Page Hampden of No. 44 squadron

The postcard sent by Don Seager whilst he was recovering in Aberystwyth Hospital after the crash. It is to Harry Moyle, a fellow observer on 44 sgn at Waddington and some of whose experiences are recounted here.

View over Aberystwyth. To the left is the monument at Pen Dinas. L4085 crashed on the extreme right of the picture.

form of an up-ended cannon set up by a local landowner who fought at Waterloo. Here you will not only have a splendid view of the area but may spare a thought for those who died on that fateful day over 30 years ago.

MR 135/532793

"Frederick Angus" the Aberystwyth lifeboat pictured in 1938. It picked up the body of one of the crew of L4085 on August 1st, 1940. It was retired in 1949.

AUGUST 1ST.—ABERYSTWYTH, CARDIGANSHIRE. At 6.30 A.M. the coastguard reported Very's lights several miles to the S.W. by W. An easterly breeze was blowing, with a smooth sea. Police helped in getting the life-boat crew assembled, and with the help of soldiers the motor life-boat *Frederick Angus* was launched at 7.26 A.M. Before the life-boat got away it was learned that an aeroplane—a Hampden bomber—was down. Aeroplanes and motor boats from Aberystwyth and New Quay took part in the search. The life-boat picked up one body and returned ashore at 12.15 P.M. Two of the aeroplane's crew were rescued by another boat. Two had lost their lives.—Rewards, £9 3s.

ABERYSTWYTH, CARDIGANSHIRE. At 9.30 in the morning of the 1st August, 1940, the coastguard asked the owner of the motor boat *Emerald Star* to go out to a spot where aircraft were searching for survivors of an aeroplane down in the sea. The weather was fine and the sea smooth. Three men put out in the motor boat. They picked up one airman alive, then another unconscious who could not be revived, and then a third who was very exhausted and whom, with much difficulty, they rescued from a rubber boat. A motor boat from New Quay also went out, and the Aberystwyth life-boat picked up the body of the fourth member of the aeroplane's crew.—Rewards, £3 7s. 6d.

Left and Right:
Extracts from RNLI records
for August 1st, 1940.

"Frederick Angus" 1993.
The original name can be seen
painted below Yr Ystwyth.

Hampden Postscript: The Pressures of War

The postcard reproduced here was written by Sgt Don Seager, whilst he was recuperating in Aberystwyth hospital, after the crash. He sent it to his fellow Observer, Sgt Harry Moyle, back at RAF Waddington. Harry tells me that when he received the card he too was in hospital and when he related the circumstances to me I felt that the reader would perhaps gain a little insight in to the pressures these young men were under during World War 2.

On December 21st, 1939 a force of 24 Hampdens and 18 Wellingtons were despatched to search for enemy shipping, but failed to locate any targets.

When the Hampdens were returning to their base in Scotland they were attacked, in error, by Spitfires of 602 'City of Glasgow' squadron and two of the aircraft, including Harry Moyle's were shot down into the sea. Harry was trapped in the aircraft when it sank and, after managing to free himself, floated in the ice-cold water for half an hour or so before being rescued.

Later, whilst flying over the North Sea, the aircraft iced-up and dropped, out of control, from 12,000 feet down to 400 feet. This frightening experience, coming on top of the shooting down, broke Harry's nerve and on a later operational flight he was shaking so much that he was unable to do his job. On going to the M.O. that Officer's, diagnosis was "cowardice" and he remarked

" . . . If I had my way you'd be shot!" As Harry says, tongue firmly in cheek, "One of life's gentlemen!" Harry was 19 at the time. After some non-operational flying, he spent the rest of the war on the ground.

His recently published book, *The Hampden File*, makes fascinating reading.

Avro Lancaster B Mk 1 W4326

The Avro Lancaster was, without a doubt, the most famous bomber to see service in the RAF. It started life as the "Manchester", a twin-engined aircraft powered by Rolls-Royce "Vulture" engines. Because of insufficient development of the engines, however, failures were so frequent as to cause the Manchester's withdrawal from service after only 18 months of operations.

When the Manchester was converted to four Rolls-Royce "Merlin" engines, to replace the "Vultures", the Lancaster was born. It had a maximum speed of 287 mph, could carry normally a 14,000 lb bomb load (although modified "Lancasters" could carry the Barnes Wallis designed 22,000 lb bomb) over 1,600 miles range and was armed with 8 0.303″ Browning machines guns in three power operated turrets. It turned out to be by far and away the most successful of the RAF's three 4 engined heavy bombers. It became famous for the Dam Busters raid, sinking the German battleship "Tirpitz", the low level flight across Germany to the M.A.N. diesel engine works at Augsburg and many other great operations. It was, to quote Sir Arthur Harris, AOC in C Bomber Command " . . . a shining sword in the hands of Bomber Command crews". Its crew won 10 VCs during the course of operations. Over 6,400 Lancasters were built, of which about half were lost on operations. Unhappily, only two Lancasters survive in flying condition today.

* * *

101 squadron operated Lancasters in 1942; later in the war this squadron's aircraft carried an eighth crew member to operate special equipment to jam German night fighter broadcasts, and its aircraft could be identified by the radio masts along the top of the fuselage. However, this was in the future; on November 16th, 1942 Lancaster W4326 piloted by Warrant Officer Spinney, a Canadian, left RAF Holme-on-Spalding Moor on a navigational exercise. Whilst flying over Wales, a photo-flash bomb ignited in the rear fuselage, blowing off the tail section. The aircraft dived into the ground on Dolwen Hill near Llangadfan, killing all on board.

* * *

This high moorland is wet and peaty so the engines dug well into the ground; Salvage teams may well have buried them deeper to avoid the difficult task of recovering them. In 1988 one of the engines was recovered, reconditioned and put on display. The site today has much identifiable wreckage including part of a crew seat, fuel tanks, an electrical panel and lots of other fragments.

W/O Spinney is buried in Tywyn Cemetery together with wireless operator Sgt Gould and the Observer Sgt Collett.

My first trip proved fruitless. The map reference appeared to be very simple, however, a couple of hours searching revealed nothing.

Next, I contacted Mr Jones, owner of Dolwen farm, who took me part of the way in his Land-Rover. Even so, a couple of hours of hard trudging through strength-sapping boggy moorland, proved unsuccessful. Returning to the farm exhausted, Mr Jones took me all the way in the Land-Rover! How I missed the site on my previous attempts is beyond me, and just goes to emphasise how important is local information, as well as a map reference.

MR 125/955092

*An Avro Lancaster
of 44 Squadron.*

*Lancaster DV302, veteran of
121 operations survived the war
only to meet its end under the
contractor's axe.*

*Below: W4326 crash site
on Dolwen Hill.*

*One of the exploded fuel tanks of
W4326 showing the singed
self-sealing material.*

Engineer's electrical panel.

*Commonwealth crew members are
buried in Tywyn Cemetery.*

Vickers-Armstrong's Wellington Mk 1C R1534

On December 20th, 1942 Plt Off. E.F. Elliott, an Australian, took off from Moreton-in-the-Marsh, Gloucestershire home of 21 OTU, on an exercise, which included, amongst other duties, a photoflash exercise over the bombing range at Radway. The wireless operator/air gunner was fatally injured when a photoflash exploded prematurely in the flare chute, although it is not certain whether he was killed immediately.* (R.D. Cooling, the Wellington pilot who lent me the photograph reproduced of Sgt H. Bean launching a flame float, tells me that crews loathed dropping the things and they gave as much fright as did the flak. They often ignited uncomfortably close to the aircraft).

The pilot ordered the other crew members to bale out, but the navigator told the pilot that he was not certain whether the W/OP was dead, but was unable to do anything to help the injured man. The navigator then baled out, and together with the other crew members who had already left the aircraft, landed safely.

*Note: Flares, flame floats & photoflashes, (a kind of bomb which emitted an intense flash of light by which photographs of the target could be taken) were launched down a long chute in the side of the fuselage, usually by the wireless operator.

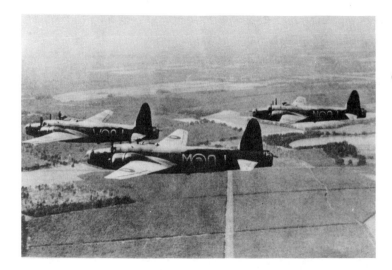

Wellington Mk. 1A s. over
East Anglia early in 1940
(OJ-W Failed to return from Ostend
September 8/9th, 1940,
OJ-N lost October 9/10th, 1940)

A wireless operator, in a posed
picture, shows how flamefloats
and flares were despatched down
the chute on the starboard side
of the aircraft.
An explosion in this chute was the
cause of the loss of R1534.

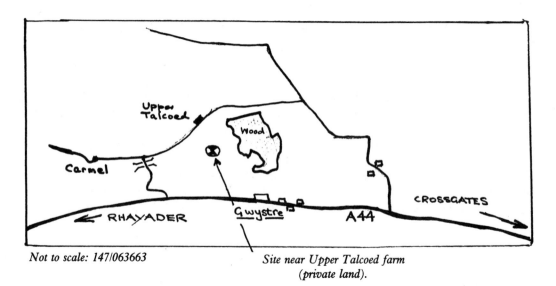

Not to scale: 147/063663

Site near Upper Talcoed farm
(private land).

Crash site at Upper Talcoed farm.

*Part of geodetic framework
taken to Brooklands Museum
for identification.*

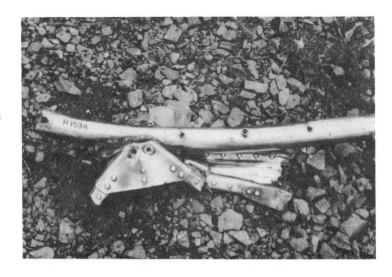

P/O Elliott was considering bailing out, but seeing some villages nearby, and with the uncertainty as to whether the W/OP was still alive, decided to remain with the aeroplane. By this time, the aircraft was down to 1,500 feet, on fire, and virtually uncontrollable, but he managed to make a successful forced landing in a field near Upper Talcoed farm near Nantmel, Radnor. On hitting the ground the aircraft immediately burst into flames and it was quite impossible to reach the injured wireless operator. The pilot was warmly praised for his dedication to duty.

This site is a fairly flat field, and so, in common with many such sites there is little, if anything to be seen. The farmer's wife was very helpful, and told me that four or so years ago, a group were searching in a particular field and got her daughter to take me there.

The metal detector brought to light much wreckage, including the front gun turret door handle and a section of a geodetic construction with the Vickers-Armstrong's '285' prefix used for the Wellington.

MR 147 063664

Armstrong-Whitworth Whitley Mk V BD232

The Carneddau range of mountains stretches from the A5 road to the South almost to Llanfairfechan. Its many peaks of over 3,000 feet presented a formidable obstacle and along its length lie the wreckage of many aircraft. Foel Fras lies about half-way down and on its lower slopes Whitley BD232 met its end.

The Whitley, together with the Hampden and Wellington, formed the mainstay of Bomber Command in the early war years and was used on most of the longer range operations, including those to northern Italy. In its earlier versions it was powered by Armstrong-Siddeley 'Tiger' radial engines but later Marks, of which BD232, was one, were fitted with the more powerful Rolls-Royce "Merlin", which gave it a top speed of 222 mph. It was armed with 5 0.303″ machine guns in two turrets and could carry a bomb load of 7,000 lb over short ranges.

Many famous bomber pilots flew the Whitley including Gp. Capt. Cheshire VC who was awarded an immediate DSO after a raid on Cologne. By 1942, however, with the introduction of more powerful aircraft into Bomber Command, the Whitley was relegated other roles: in Coastal Command, for parachuting and as a trainer.

On the night of September 26th, 1942, BD232, with Sgt Stuart (RNZAF) as pilot, took off on a night cross-country exercise over the Irish Sea, from 24 OTU Honeybourne, near Evesham. After a radio check from the aircraft shortly after 1900 hours, nothing further was heard.

Believing that the aircraft had probably come down in the sea, a search was soon initiated but nothing was found. Next day with improving weather conditions, an aircraft from Honeybourne commenced a search of the route, eventually spotting what appeared to be a Whitley in the Carneddau, near Llyn Dulyn; all the crew had perished. (After this accident aircraft were re-routed to the north to avoid this hazard).

As an aside, it should be remembered that, even in daylight, should an aircraft break cloud in a mountainous region much below the surrounding peaks, with a climb rate of only 800 feet per minute, there is little chance of gaining sufficient height to escape. Compare this with the Canberra bomber, which first flew less than 6 years later and climbs at 3,700 fpm. Such is the power of the modern jet engine.

* * *

The walk to the site should be easy. About an hour or so travelling due west from the nearest track. However, I am worried about a river shown on the map, which, after the preceding day's heavy rain, might prove to be difficult.

The first half-hour presents no problems, other than that is across boggy ground. The river, however, as expected, is quite high and the rocks slippery. I decide to jump over, but with haversack, camera and it has to be said, a little too much on the waistline, I end up with both feet trailing in the rushing waters. Next, a short climb, past a copse of trees and then, with the rock face in view and the wreckage sighted, a final obstacle — 250 yards of bog! I decide to go more westerly, towards the lake and skirt around it. Llyn Dulyn, the *Black Lake*, is sombre and brooding. Behind it the rock face goes up sheer to 2,000 feet and the wind is whipping up the surface of the water; waterfalls cascade into it from the rocks above. I remember that in this inhospitable place, in 1944, an American C-47 (Dakota) crashed into the rock face, killing all on board; most of the wreckage now lies on the lake bed where it has fallen.

The superhuman efforts made by the RAF men from Llandrog to reach the wreckage were such that the future of the RAF Mountain Rescue Service, formed in the area only months earlier, was secure.

Ten minutes scrambling over the rocks and the wreckage is easily located. The wind is near gale force and a couple of times I am blown off my feet, as I hop from rock to rock, narrowly missing breaking my camera.

The wreckage is well spread down the hillside and, although various groups have recovered many items, parts of the rear turret, flap mechanism and a "Merlin" crankshaft still bear grim testament to the tragedy which occurred 50 years ago.

I offer a silent prayer for those who died.

MR 115/703671

*Armstrong-Whitworth
Whitley Mk. V*

Rolls-Royce Merlin crankshaft

*Above: Wreckage on Foel Fras
with Llyn Dulyn, the Black Lake,
in the background.*

*Propeller reduction gearing
and remains of wooden blade.*

Handley-Page Halifax B Mk V LL541

Gerald Lister was born in Amherst Nova Scotia, Canada on January 18, 1922. When he was 17 he started work as an aero-engine mechanic at the Canadian Car Co., at that time an aircraft manufacturing plant. In August 1942 he joined the RCAF and started the long process of becoming a pilot at No. 12 Elementary Flying Training School, Gooderick on Tiger Moths and later at Camp Bowren on the Harvard where, in November 1943, he completed the course and was awarded his pilot's flying badge as a Temporary Sergeant.

He left Halifax by sea in March 1944, arriving in the UK 8 days later. Posted to Kidlington near Oxford for multi-engine training, he passed out an 'Average' pilot on the Airspeed Oxford with 64 flying hours on type. On then to 82 OTU Ossington near Newark, where 77 flying hours on Wellingtons were added to his rapidly mounting total, before moving on to 1664 HCU Dishforth, York for crewing up for the final phase of training.

He had by now been promoted to Pilot Officer and his crew consisted:

Plt. Off.	LISTER	Pilot
Fg. Off.	BRAUTIGAN	Navigator
Sgt	LEVINE	Bomb Aimer
Sgt	PREECE	W/OP
Sgt	WILLMEK	Flt. Engineer
Sgt	OVERLAND	Mid-upper gunner
Sgt	GOEHRING	Rear gunner

although on December 12th, 1944 an extra engineer Sgt McMurtry joined the crew.

★ ★ ★

December 12th, 1944 was a cloudy day with little wind but with light showers passing over. Plt. Off. Lister and his crew took-off in LL541 coded ZU-O on a practice cross-country and bombing exercise at 1010 in the morning, at about the same time as another Halifax, ZU-K piloted by Fg. Off. Mutch.

At about 1300 hours whilst flying over Wales at 18,000 feet, Sgt Whiteside, the mid-upper gunner of ZU-K observed LL541 flying astern of them at about 3-4,000 yards, when it dropped a wing as if to start a corkscrew manoeuvre; from there it went into a vertical dive recovering some 3,000 feet below. It then nosed down continuing its dive, disappearing into the cloud, the top of which was at about 8,000 feet. The aircraft emerged from the cloud at about 3,000 feet where it was seen by Mr T.C. Price of the Royal Observer Corps who stated that it was still in a vertical dive and before it crashed, what appeared to be parts of the aircraft were falling around it. The aircraft hit the ground and disintegrated killing all the occupants.

Handley-Page Halifax

Plt. Off. Lister, taken on his first joining the RCAF

One of the main impact points.

The later enquiry could not establish the cause of the accident, other then suggesting oxygen failure affecting the pilot. Although there was major structural failure in the air, the aircraft did not catch fire. As it is not known whether later investigations by the Accident Investigation Branch came to any other conclusions, this accident has many similarities to that of LW366 (page 80). Possibly the initial recovery at 15,000 feet damaged the elevator controls whereupon the aircraft fell out of control.

LL541 was one of a batch manufactured by Rootes Securities of Speke, Liverpool. 1664 HCU at Dishforth was converting to Mark III Halifaxes later than month. (Paradoxically, the earlier Mark number was an improved version, which often happened in the aircraft industry when an advanced design took longer to develop than was initially planned, and an interim aircraft came into service with a later Mark number.)

★ ★ ★

The site is not too far from Rhayader on the A44 but is on high boggy terrain and is subject to quickly changeable weather conditions. Indeed, I went up for the first time in bright sunshine, only to return, after finding nothing, two hours later in a snow-storm. The wreckage is well spread around but concentrated in four or so areas. Because of the growth of heather over the years, thousands of parts are probably hidden and will never be found. Most of the more interesting pieces have long gone; an "enthusiast" in Rhayader has shown me hundreds of pieces, while some interesting items are to be seen in Rhayader's small museum. However, the area is still littered with thousands of fragments, many having the prefix "57" (Handley-Page design 57). I also found a number of Rolls-Royce "Merlin" valves, complete with springs and a number of parts incorporating quite large pieces of timber.

MR 147/930667

Wreckage on Nant-yr-Haidd.

Hawker Hunter F6 XJ635

The Hawker Hunter was possibly the most beautiful single-engined jet fighter to see service. It was powered by one 10,000 lb thrust Rolls-Royce Avon turbojet engine and reached a speed of 715 mph at sea level. It was armed with 4 30mm Aden cannon, with provision for bombs and rockets under the wings. Strangely enough, it came from the same stable as the 'Hurricane', whereas Supermarine, designers of the incomparable 'Spitfire', produced the rather ugly 'Swift'. The Hunter first flew in July 1951 and remained in squadron service for 20 years.

Prior to the formation of the famous 'Red Arrows', No. 111 squadron provided the RAF's aerobatic team with the superb 'Black Arrows' and the author was lucky enough to be one those present at the 1958 Farnborough Air Show when they performed a formation loop with 22 aircraft. The Hunter was exported to many countries and indeed, a number are still flying in the UK.

* * *

On May 4th, 1976, Fg. Off. Irvin took-off from the Tactical Weapons Unit, Brawdy at 0830 hrs for a low-level cross-country check. He was accompanied by a staff instructor in another aircraft.

After crossing the coast inbound, north of Aberystwyth they encountered low cloud at about 500 feet. Fg. Off. Irvin told the instructor that he was going to climb above the cloud. The instructor told him, over the radio, to return independently and that he, the instructor, would continue at low level.

On entering cloud in the climb, Fg. Off. Irvin became disoriented, emerging from the cloud at about 450 knots and at an angle from which recovery was impossible. (Often whilst in thick cloud, or in Arctic conditions where there seems to be no differentiation between sky and land, it is difficult, without reference to instruments, to know which way is "up"). He immediately initiated ejection procedures but, by this time, the aircraft was very close to the ground. The seat ejected but the drogue had, inevitably, only partially deployed when the seat and its occupant hit the ground. The pilot was killed instantly. The aircraft exploded and pieces were thrown into nearby fields.

* * *

The farmer, Mr Scott, told me that the salvage crews spent 3 weeks clearing the area, and that the field had been ploughed three times since the crash. The chances of locating any fragments would be remote. With the co-operation of the owner of the adjacent farm, Mrs Sarah Davies, I spent two hours combing the area without success, until it occurred to me that, as the crash happened in May, when the hedgerows were in full leaf, fragments may have been blown into the thick, prickly, hawthorns, and may have been overlooked. It was now January and the branches were bare, perhaps I might find something there.

After much scratching, (of my face and hands!) I noticed a piece of metal protruding through the moss. I managed to get into the hedge and, on scraping away a great deal of undergrowth, discovered about a score of pieces in quite a concentrated area. These consisted of two sections of turbine rings, complete with blades, part of the cockpit area, with ejection seat markings and many unidentifiable pieces of structure. Further search revealed nothing else.

Mrs Davies told me that the parents of Fg. Off. Irvin came up to the site about a year after the crash, and said that it gave them some sort of peace to see where their son had died. They gave Mrs Davies a photograph of their son, which I was privileged to see, and they subsequently wrote a letter to her thanking her for her kindness to them.

MR 135/618794

A Hawker Hunter of the famous 'Black Arrows' aerobatic team of 111 squadron.

Pilot of XJ635 Fg. Off. Winton Irvine seen here at Linton-on-Ouse in January 1975 on the day he qualified as a pilot in the RAF (Photo by permission of Mrs K.F. Irvine)

Fragment of XJ635 showing ejector seat markings.

Crash site at Moriah. The ejector seat hit the ground on the left of the picture. The aircraft crashed towards the hedge on the right of the picture, bringing down the power lines.

Vickers-Armstrong's Wellington GR Mk VIII LB185

The Wellington, in addition to its bomber role, was also used as a General Reconnaissance aircraft by Coastal Command. At one time thirteen squadrons were so equipped. The mark VIII was the first to be fitted with ASV (Air to Surface Vessel radar) with a line of masts along the top of the rear fuselage. Some were also fitted with powerful searchlights to illuminate U-boats on the surface recharging their batteries at night; 394 Mark VIIIs were built, their performance similar to the Mark I.

No. 3 OTU near Haverfordwest, was a Coastal Command training until and crews made a number of long flights from there during their training to prepare them for the extended patrols they would be doing on posting to an operational squadron.

On November 19th, 1943, Sgt Wolman took-off in LB185 for a night cross-country flight. During the flight, whilst flying over unbroken cloud and mist, the radio became unserviceable. At about 2 in the morning, after being airborne for about 6 hours and with the fuel state becoming critical, the pilot decided that he had to descend to try and fix their position.

The aircraft was still in thick fog when it struck the 1500 foot Moel-y-Croeso, a high boggy heathland south of Ffestiniog. Four of the crew of six were killed instantly.

The WOP AG Sgt Sinclair found the other gunner Sgt Maskell, up to his chest in the boggy ground and could not extricate him. He then struggled down the hillside in the cold, foggy November night finally reaching Bwlch Gwyn farmhouse over four hours later. The farmer, Mr Roberts could not go for help himself having injured his legs in a motorcycle accident. However, help was sent for, and a party of men went up to the site and stayed until the Mountain Rescue team arrived to extricate Sgt Maskell who had spinal injuries. Sgt Lauritz, a member of the crew who died in the crash is buried in Chester cemetery.

* * *

On going to the site, I stopped to confirm that I was taking the right road and by one of those strange coincidences the man I spoke to was Gwyn Jones. A nineteen year old at the time, he was living in Cae Glas farm adjacent to Bwlch Gwyn and he has vivid memories of that day. He went up to the site with the Station Master from Trawsfynydd, the doctor from the nearby army camp and a couple of others. It was still foggy and Sgt Sinclair was not certain whether he had crossed one or two streams on his way down. However, the site was found and the young Gwyn was shocked by the human remains scattered around. The doctor gave first aid to Sgt Maskell but could not move him because of his injuries and shortly after 10 am the Mountain Rescue team arrived. Gwyn remembers them with a smile, "very well turned out they were, with good boots and nice white socks."

* * *

The route to the site is up a well-defined track. After a short climb, a bare, featureless moor is reached, relieved only by two bright green fields with a derelict farmhouse nearby. This is Dolddinas where Sgt Sinclair rested on his way down from the crash. Passing the farm, the abandoned gold mine comes into view but nothing remains save the empty shell of the men's barracks. No going home at night for the miners in those days; the nearest habitation was at Trawsfynydd about 5 miles away. The mine finally closed in 1939.

A few hundred yards beyond the mine, virtually underneath the pylons which march across the moor from Trawsfynydd nuclear power station, a large rocky outcrop can be seen to the left of the track; LB185 crashed here. Most large wreckage has gone, but small fragments abound and pieces of geodetics, with discernible part numbers are in evidence.

MR124/747386

A Wellington GR Mk. 8 after a minor mishap. The Air-to-Surface Vessel radar masts can be seen mounted on the rear fuselage.

LB185 crashed into this hill on top of Moel-y-Croeso. The bog where Sgt Maskell was trapped is in the foreground.

View down from Moel-y-Croeso. Dolddinas farm where Sgt Sinclair rested is in the centre of the picture.

Gwyn Jones also remembers the day he took a small child for a walk up a hill behind the farm, when through the clouds a Dornier 215 twin-engined bomber appeared, hotly pursued by a Spitfire which promptly shot it down. It crashed in the lane leading to Tyddyn Sais farm at Trawsfynydd. The next day the wreckage was put on display, a collection being made for the local Wings for Victory campaign. Whilst the wreckage was being inspected by all and sundry, someone moved some equipment, there was a bang and a bullet hit a bystander in the leg.

Thus, a Trawsfynydd inhabitant was injured by a German bullet fired some 24 hours after the aircraft had crashed and the surviving crew members carted off to a prison camp!*

As the farm lane has been raised by about 10 feet during the construction of the new main road, no sign of this crash remains.

MR 124/709333

Small wreckage with paint still adhering to it.

Dornier 215 VB+KK crashed into this field.

* A gunner of the Do215 crew, Gustav Pelzer, was the first German airman to be buried in Wales in WW2.

De Havilland Mosquito FB6 HX862

The De Havilland Mosquito was one of the most important British aircraft of the Second World War. Constructed mainly of laminated wood, a plywood/balsa sandwich, many components were made not by engineering companies as was the case with conventional aircraft, but by the furniture industry around High Wycombe not too far from the De Havilland works at Hatfield.

As a bomber it was so fast that it needed no defensive armament, and photographic reconnaissance variants could exceed 400 mph. The fighter-bomber version, the FB6, was armed with 4 20 mm cannon, 4 0.303" machine guns and could carry a 2000 lb bomb load over a range of 1200 miles. It was powered by two Rolls-Royce Merlin engines of 1230 hp each and could attain 380 mph.

The Mosquito took part in many important low-level attacks, notably the breaching of the prison walls at Amiens, where the leader Gp. Capt. Pickard DSO, DFC lost his life. (As Flt Lt Pickard he starred in the morale boosting film of 1941 "Target for Tonight"). Mosquitos were also responsible for the destruction of the Gestapo Headquarters in Copenhagen. It was also used by Wg. Cdr. Cheshire DSO of 617 Squadron (later Gp. Capt. Cheshire VC founder of the Cheshire Homes) to mark targets at low level giving much greater accuracy.

An OTU for training Mosquito crews was at High Ercall a few miles from a well-known Shropshire landmark, The Wrekin, near Wellington.

On September 25th, 1944 P.O. Else, with Flt Lt Johnson as his navigator took-off on a night navigational exercise. They appeared to have strayed off course and descended through cloud over the Carneddau range, hitting the side of Drum at about 2250 feet above sea level. The crew were killed outright. The Royal Observer Corps notified their controller that the aircraft had crashed at 0045 hours and the wreckage was found by local searchers at 0830.

★ ★ ★

I walk for nearly two hours through mist and low cloud. Gaps in the cloud reveal distant views to the South, one row of mountains superimposed on another disappearing into the mist. Foel Grach stands with its peak covered with a halo of cloud, an occasional shaft of sunlight lighting the scene.

Farmers are very fond of using old bedsteads as fence post substitutes, but the fence here is a masterpiece of improvisation; there must be about 100 bedstead rails in one stretch. How they got up the side of a Welsh mountain is anyone's guess.

The wreckage of HX862 on the cloud-covered slopes of Drum.

De Havilland
Mosquito FB6

The final bomber version
of the Mosquito; B Mk 35

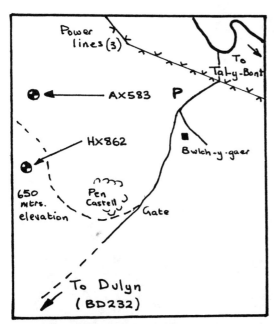

——— Track   – – – Footpath

Not to scale

The wreckage is in an East facing fully, undercarriage parts the first to be seen, badly corroded, plenty of wood screws (the Mosquito was known as the "Wooden Wonder" by the way) quite a few panels with plywood fragments attached, and one tiny fragment of wood with the fabric covering still sticking to it and the paint showing it to have been in day type camouflage. (The skinning of the Mosquito was screwed and nailed into place and then covered with doped fabric.)

As the crow flies, this site is only about half a mile from the crash site of Anson AX583.

Bristol Beaufighter TF X RD210

The Bristol Beaufighter which first flew in 1939, was a powerful twin engined aircraft, capable of well over 300 mph. It proved to be an excellent night-fighter and anti-shipping strike aircraft. The Mark X version was powered by two Bristol Hercules engines, of 1772 hp each, and could attain 303 mph.

No. 1 Ferry Unit of 44 Group Maintenance Command at Pershore, Worcs. had the responsibility of delivering RD 210 and it is most likely that it was destined for use overseas. Because of this it was necessary to conduct a fuel consumption test, as no two aircraft use the same amount of fuel and, as a flight to a unit abroad may involve a longish sea crossing, might well be crucial.

Flt Lt A.L. Roe, with W/O. Newbry as navigator, was detailed to carry out this test on February 10th, 1945, and briefed not to continue if cloud and icing conditions were encountered. It is thought that the pilot took action to avoid a storm and in so doing entered cloud and struck Aran Fawddwy, in Meirionnydd, at 2793 feet. Both crew members were killed.

★ ★ ★

The Mark 10 Bristol Beaufighter.

Aran Fawddwy: Point of impact.

*Bristol Hercules engine and
other wreckage in lake.*

Bristol Hercules XVII, 1772 hp

*Engine and propeller
reduction gearing.*

Getting to the site involves very hard walking for a couple of hours (each way) across boggy, undulating terrain. The mountain is behind the lake, Craiglyn Dyfi, the wreckage being scattered from the point of impact, high on the mountain, all the way down and into the lake. The most recognisable parts are, the two engines and the propeller reduction gears. I climbed up towards the point of impact, but a little over three quarters of the way up, decided that the loose, heavy, overhanging rocks made further progress hazardous and so was forced to make a somewhat frustrated descent.

As the remains of a P51, P47 and a Mosquito are scattered around Aran Fawddwy, a return trip is indicated, but it would be a good idea to look at a couple of sites on lower ground first to get the calf muscles back into trim.

MR 124/863226

Flight to Disaster: The Story of Three Spitfires
Vickers-Armstrong's Supermarine Spitfire Mk VB:
R7296, BL518, BM573

The Spitfire is, without doubt the most famous aircraft of all time. Designed by Reginald Mitchell it was a direct descendant of the seaplanes which won the Schneider Trophy outright for Britain in 1931. It first flew in March 1936, and was an immediate success. Powered by a Rolls-Royce "Merlin" engine of 1030 hp it could attain a speed of 355 mph and carried an armament of eight 0.303″ Browning machine guns.

In the Battle of Britain, although considerably outnumbered by the Hurricane, the Spitfires excellent performance, coupled with its beauty of line, immediately caught the public imagination and assured its place in the history books.

During the course of the war, over 20,000 Spitfires were built, its speed during this time increasing from 355 mph to 460 mph.

The Mark V version was built to counter the improved performance of German fighters; its speed was upped to 374 mph and the armament uprated by fitting two 20mm cannon, in addition to four 0.303″ machine guns. Over 6,000 Mark Vs were built and it was widely used until it too needed improvement. In July 1942 it was superceded by the Mark IX.

★ ★ ★

RAF Llanbedr, near Harlech, is still an airfield today. During the war it was used mainly by squadrons on detachment for air-to-air and air-to-ground firing practice, although it did have its resident fighter squadron. In August 1942 41 squadron, commanded by Sqn Ldr G. Hyde, took up residence at Llanbedr but, shortly after their arrival, they were despatched to Southern England to take part in the ill-fated raid on Dieppe. Heavy losses were sustained by all of those involved during this testing of the German defences and 41 squadron returned sadly to Llanbedr after losing the C.O. and five other pilots.

On October 22nd, 1942 three Spitfires of 'A' Flight, R7296, BL518 and BM573, flown by Flt Lt Gillet, P.O. Harrison and P.O. Scott took-off on a formation flying exercise. Shortly after, they entered cloud and, before they could climb through it, they struck the western slopes of Tarrenhendre mountain. The pilots were all killed instantly. As soon as radio contact was lost, aircraft from Llanbedr searched the area without success, and it was assumed that they had crashed into the sea, perhaps as a result of a collision. The wreckage was not found until two days later.

★ ★ ★

As the history of the Spitfire is well documented, it is possible to trace these aircraft from the factory to the windswept Welsh hillside where they met their end.

R7296 was the oldest. It was manufactured at the old Supermarine works at Woolston, Southampton and made its first flight from nearby Eastleigh on April 3rd, 1941. It was named "Newbury II". It was the practice to name aircraft after towns which had made collections in "Wings for Victory" weeks. (The cost of a Spitfire was quoted at the time as £5,000!) After its first flight it went to No. 9 Maintenance Unit and thence to 91, 611, 64 and 317 squadrons before being allocated to 41 squadron.

BL518 was made at the vast "shadow" factory at Castle Bromwich and was delivered to 5 MU on December 12th, 1941. It served with 313, 154 and 71 squadrons before ending up on 41.

BM573 was the newest, being delivered to the RAF on May 2nd, 1942. Another Castle Brom aircraft, it only served with 610 squadron before going to 41. It survived only 5 months from factory to its tragic end.

★ ★ ★

Left: Spitfire Mark Vbs

Right: Spitfire Vb AB910 which is still flying. This aircraft once took-off with Margaret Horton of the WAAF clinging to the tail. She was lucky to survive the experience.

Above: Fragment of Rolls-Royce Merlin cooling system found on Tarrenhendre and, Right: where it fits on the front of the engine between the banks of cylinders.

Tarrenhendre can be approached either from Pennal, on the A493 Aberdyfi road, or from Dolgoch, on the B4405 Talyllyn road. Whichever way is chosen it is a hard, uphill walk, tiring for all but the fittest. The advantage of a Dolgoch start is that a clearly defined track takes you most of the way. When it ends it is but a short distance along the contours, rather than further uphill. The terrain is heather covered and lumpy, hard to walk over and even harder to search. Given a little effort, though, something should be found. Recent trips have produced part of the glycol header tank, a fragment of rudder bar (with Spitfire '300' marking) and part of the "Merlin" engine plumbing.

However, unless you are lucky enough to find something with a serial number on it you will be unable to tell from which aircraft it comes.

MR 135/675035

*Cloud sweeps up the valley
onto Tarrenhendre.*

*View across the River Dyfi with
Tarrenhendre to the left covered
by cloud.*

Vickers-Armstrong's Wellington Mk 1C X9666

The outbreak of the war in Europe brought men to Britain from all parts of the world to fight in the cause of freedom. As well as having their own squadrons in Bomber Command, men from the Commonwealth and from Occupied Europe were to be found in all RAF squadrons. However, the pilot of X9666 must be unusual as he came from Buenos Aires, in the Argentine.

So sad that his efforts should have ended on a mist-covered Welsh hillside.

* * *

On the last day of 1943, Wellington X9666 took off from Moreton-in-the-Marsh, Gloucestershire for a typical cross-country flight over Wales, which included a bombing exercise near Aberdyfi.

The crew were:

Pilot	:	Fg. Off. C. Amos
Navigator	:	Sgt T. Freeman
WOP/AG.	:	Sgt T. Briggs
Bomb Aimer	:	Sgt P. North
Rear Gunner	:	Sgt A. Mandell

After completing the bombing practice they crossed the mist covered coast just north of Borth, at around 2000 feet. If their timings had been correct at this stage a descent would have been quite safe as, at this point, the Dovey estuary is about 3 miles wide, if the Fochno bog is included. (They would still have had to alter course to port, or climb again very quickly if disaster was to be averted.) Seeing a gap in the layer of cloud which stretched before them, the pilot descended through it. By this time, however, they had crossed the estuary and were approaching the northern bank of the Dyfi, (indeed, the Bomb Aimer, Sgt North, who survived the crash said later that he glimpsed the estuary through the cloud over the pilot's shoulder, flying at around 1000 feet). It appears that the aircraft was being banked sharply to port, the pilot may well have seen the rising ground in front of him, when the port wing struck the ground above Aberdyfi. The fuselage broke in two and the aircraft caught fire. Only two of the crew survived: the Bomb Aimer, Sgt North, and the Rear Gunner, Sgt Mandell. The latter was rescued by a local youth and taken to Tywyn Hospital, most probably owing his life to the fact that the rear of the aircraft became broken away from the rest of the wreckage.

The Pilot, Fg. Off. Amos, now rests in Tywyn Cemetery. In 1992, nearly 50 years after the tragedy and after years of effort, an aviation historian, Eddie Doylerush, managed to bring the two survivors and their rescuers together at the site, above Aberdyfi.

* * *

The site is easily approached by a minor road, rising uphill from Aberdyfi. At the top, the view from the ridge is stunning. The Dyfi estuary provides a spectacular back-drop while, to the north, a green valley is dotted with white farmsteads. Originally known as Cwm Dyffryn its name was known to the English as Happy Valley when the railway brought a vast influx of Victorian tourists to the area. After crossing a cattle grid a second faint track heads off to the right and takes us to the site. With marshy ground on two sides this lies in a small field, approached through a gate.

After obtaining permission from the farmer, the field may be searched but there is little hope of finding anything after all these years.

On a quiet winter's day when looking out to sea one can almost hear the engines of the aircraft as it approaches through the mist.

MR 135/632977

The crash site of X9666 viewed from Llancynfelin across the Dyfi estuary. The aircraft crashed in the field to the right of the light coloured field in the centre of the photograph.

X9666 Approached over Dyfi bar.

Lockheed P38G Lightning 42-13345

The Lightning was unusual for Allied fighters of the period in being a twin-boom design with the pilot and armament housed in a central pod. It was powered by two Allison in-line engines of 1600 hp each and, unlike many twin-engined fighters, was well able to take care of itself in fighter-to-fighter combat. It was used, together with the P51 Mustang and P47 Thunderbolt by the Eighth Air Force to escort formations of heavy bombers deep into Germany.

A version of the P38 was used for photographic reconnaissance and designated the F5 but there is no evidence available now to show that 42-13345 was one of these other than the fact that it belonged to the 27th PR squadron at Chalgrove, Oxfordshire.

★ ★ ★

On September 11th, 1945 Lt Xenophon Eugenides took-off on a training flight which took him over Wales. What happened there is mostly conjecture, but it appears that he crossed the coast inbound, that is to say travelling in an easterly direction at around Borth, near Aberystwyth. His flight planning must have shown that the highest ground on this leg was in the Pumlumon range, and he was at nearly 2500 feet in cloud when the aircraft just struck the summit of Pumlumon Fawr. Both propellers were sheared off and the aircraft continued, powerless, descending sharply, crashing into the hillside on the other side of the valley, killing the pilot. A possible cause for this accident could have been an incorrect altimeter setting.

P.C. Edwards from Devil's Bridge joined in the search and a shepherd, John James from Nantymoch, found the pilot dead not far from the wreckage. The ambulance was summoned, but night had fallen before it drove away taking the body to Aberystwyth mortuary. According to eye witnesses, mist on the day brought visibility down to almost nil.

★ ★ ★

Up to a few years ago this was one of the most complete aircraft crash sites in Wales. The proximity to the tourist attraction of Pumlumon has proved unfortunate. I have been told of so called 'recovery groups' removing large items only to sell them later for scrap. Nevertheless, a large amount of identifiable wreckage still remains. The left-hand boom section lies there, complete with turbo-charger and, a little further down the hill, a piece of the right-hand boom, plus engine panels that can be identified by close examination of photographs of the P38.

My first two attempts produced nothing; it is amazing how, when in the hills, one can pass within yards of a crash site and not see anything. Indeed, on my third attempt, I only found it by sheer luck.

It is a sobering thought that had Lt Eugenides been flying just 10 feet higher, he may well have been with us today.

MR 135/798870

General view of wreckage

Turbo-charger of port engine

Section of port boom. The pipe in the foreground is attached to the exhaust and leads to the turbo-charger. The piece to the left is the wing section which joins onto the fuselage.

Hawker Hunter T7 XL575

On November 8th, 1971, Hunter XL575, of No. 229 OCU RAF Chivenor, N. Devon, took-off on a live firing exercise at Pembrey ranges with Flt Lt John Metcalfe (31) as instructor and a student of the Singapore Armed Forces, 2nd Lt Bertram Yong (20) as student pilot.

Just before 13:00 hours, flying near Devil's Bridge in atrocious weather conditions, with thunder and hail, the aircraft descended at a steep angle and, at high speed, slicing through the tops of the trees in the forest adjacent to Gelmast farm, struck the ground and exploded. The wreckage scattered down through the forest, which is on a steep hillside and some fell into fields of the farm. A number of trees were burning; pieces of wreckage outside the forest were on fire. The engine appears to have disintegrated, but two large parts came to rest in the nearby fields, many yards from the impact point. 30mm ammunition was scattered over the area. Shortly after the crash, another aircraft was heard circling overhead, so perhaps two aircraft were engaged on the exercise. A forestry worker, having his lunch nearby, said that he saw a great fireball in the sky, lending weight to the theory that the aircraft had been struck by lightning. As the crash occurred within a few hundred yards from the edge of the forest, where there is a clearing with a few fields and a large farmhouse, the emergency services were able to gain access quite easily. This was only as far as recovery of the aircraft was concerned as, unfortunately, there was no hope of survival for the crew.

* * *

At 12:57 hours on November 8th, 1971, John Postings and his wife were sitting in the kitchen of Gelmast farm. The weather outside was appalling; thunder echoing around the hills and rattling the roof. There was a sudden, massive thunderclap and the flames in the kitchen range billowed out through the door of the grate. The dog leapt onto the window ledge in an excited state.

Thinking that a thunderbolt or meteor had crashed to earth, John and his wife went outside into the storm. Through the gloom they could see nothing at first, but going to the end of the farm yard they saw the trees blazing and pieces of burning wreckage littered around the fields. John went back to the house, asked for 999 on the phone and when the operator asked "Which service?" said that he didn't quite know, but that an aircraft had crashed onto his farm. In a short time the police, fire service and ambulance arrived; although after looking at the scene, both ambulance crews left as the crew were beyond help.

An RAF helicopter had been despatched to the Tregaron home of the Aberporth medical officer and landed in a field near the farmhouse.

Later on, things were not helped by a power cut, thought to have been caused by the storm. Next day, the road to the farm was blocked by local sightseers, although, as the roads are private, the police had little difficulty dispersing them, in order to let official vehicles through.

Helicopters continued to come and go, often with some difficulty, until the sheep could be rounded up. Medical staff were collecting the remains of the crew; this part of the operation being particularly harrowing, according to John Postings, as they were dividing them into "European" and "Oriental" containers.

Another concern was the large amount of 30mm ammunition scattered around; because of the pine needles and undergrowth this was hard to locate. One round was found lodged in the wall of the outside toilet.

As the farmhouse is quite large, John was able to give overnight accommodation for some of the many visitors who arrived. One of these was a Flight Lieutenant who made an investigation of the crash site. He stayed overnight, and when telephoning the base the next day, John overheard him say that he thought the aircraft had struck the ground at an angle of 40°, at about 400 mph.

A salvage team from RAF Bicester, (the author's old unit) arrived, under Sgt "Dutch" Holland and they set about collecting the thousands of pieces which had been scattered by the explosion. It was discovered that, at the point of impact, there had been a large rock which had, unbelievably, been split in two by the force of the crash. One piece, weighing a considerable amount, had been thrown a couple of hundred yards onto a track near the farmhouse. The salvage team lived in the farmhouse during this period, and others from Bicester came for shorter periods. John remembers them with some affection, despite the intervening twenty years.

He was asked to attend the inquest at RAF Chivenor, which was rather exciting for him, as he had never been to an operational flying unit before. His excitement was, however, somewhat tempered by meeting the wife and brother of the RAF pilot. Since then the brother has visited the farm, but that was many years ago.

★ ★ ★

Despite a number of new trees being planted at the site since the crash, it still has great interest. Many pieces of wreckage must have been covered by pine needles and caught up in the branches at the time. These have been brought to light by the influence of wind and rain, so that many hundreds of fragments litter the forest.

Left: An early model Hunter showing its superb lines.

Below left: A Hunter T7 similar to XL575. Note the side-by-side seating for instructor and pupil.

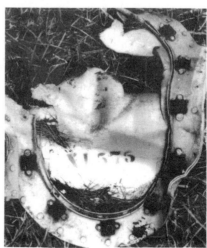

Starboard fuel tank panel.

An interesting find of mine, was the starboard wing fuel valve panel, with paint in excellent condition and with the aircraft number stencilled on the inside. Ejector seat parts and turbine blades were also seen (but not removed) together with some fuselage skinning painted "Mark 6", which is interesting, as the T7 shared many parts with the F6.

The serial number shows this to be one of a batch (probably No. 13) manufactured by Hawkers at Kingston-on-Thames. The aircraft type and mark entered service at 229 OCU some 13 years earlier. To return to the crash itself, with help from the farmer, I was able to locate the exact point of impact. The angle at which the aircraft had descended being determined by the area of new trees in front and behind

Rear entrance of Gelmast farm.
Aircraft crashed where highest tree
is on horizon.

Wreckage scattered through forest.

the spot. The area was replanted by the Forestry Commission at, according to John Postings, a cost of £2,000. It is therefore much different from the older, surrounding trees.

This was the first time for nearly thirty years that I had been to the crash site of a jet fighter; the amount and dispersal of the wreckage grim testimony to the fierceness of the explosive impact.

MR 135/775758

Lockheed Hudson III V9127

A development of the Lockheed Electra airliner, the Hudson was used by the RAF mainly in the Maritime reconnaissance role although later in the war it was also used as a transport and for training. When the British Purchasing Commission in the USA placed an order in 1938 for 250 aircraft worth $25 million it was the largest order ever taken by an American aircraft company. It was powered by two 1100 hp Wright Cyclone radial engines giving it a top speed of nearly 250 mph and a range of 2160 miles. It was armed with up to seven 0.303″ machine guns and could carry a bomb load of 750 lbs.

The Hudson had a number of "firsts" to its credit. It was the first American aircraft to see operational service with the RAF in the Second World War; it was the first RAF aircraft in the UK to shoot down an enemy aircraft: (Dornier 18 flying boat on October 8th, 1939), and was the first and most probably the last, to have a U-boat surrender to it. (U-570).

Over 2000 Hudsons were supplied to the RAF; at first they were delivered by sea, but after November 1940, all aircraft were flown across the Atlantic.

★ ★ ★

*Lockheed Hudson with its
British made Boulton & Paul
rear gun turret.*

*The crash site. Its proximity to the
new A44 road can be seen.*

No. 1 Ferry Training Unit at Honeybourne, Worcestershire was set up to train ferry crews for this and other ferrying tasks. On February 9th, 1942, Fg. Off. Anderson (RAAF) air tested Hudson V9127 at Kemble and later that day flew it to Honeybourne. The next day, together with three other crew members, he took-off on a navigation and fuel consumption test over Wales. At low altitude and in cloud, the aircraft struck rising ground to the west of the Pumlumon range near Ponterwyd. There were no survivors and the pilot and navigator are buried in Aberystwyth Cemetery.

* * *

The site is only 100 yards off the main A44 road and its accessibility has meant that virtually all wreckage has now been removed. Diligent searching, however, may well reveal small fragments, with the occasional serial number, plus a few cartridge cases.

The opportunity should not be missed, whilst parked here to visit the Nant-yr-arian forest only 200 yards away, with its lovely walks and stunning views right out to sea at Aberystwyth. A direction from which many of the aircraft that appear in these pages came.

MR 135 720812

Bad Night for Ninety-six
Boulton-Paul Defiant T4008 and N1595

The first RAF fighter in service to have a 4-gun power-operated gun turret as its sole armament, the Defiant only saw service as a day fighter in the hands of 264 squadron, where it had a great initial success; the enemy, when "bouncing" the formation, didn't expect to be met by fire from the rear of the aircraft. After this first success, the enemy didn't take long to revise their tactics, attacking from the front where the Defiant was defenceless. It was withdrawn from front line service but then enjoyed a new lease of life as a night fighter. (Somewhat similarly to the German BF 110, a rather poor day fighter in the Battle of Britain, which turned out to be probably the greatest night fighter of all time). As a night fighter, the Defiant saw service with some 13 squadrons; with its Rolls Royce Merlin XX engine of 1260 bhp, maximum speed of 315 mph and pleasant flying characteristics it was popular with its pilots and gunners.

★ ★ ★

November 3rd, 1941 was not a particularly happy night for 96 squadron, with two aircraft crashing and another being badly damaged in a forced landing. Luckily, the only injury was sustained by an air gunner who suffered a broken ankle.

Sqn Ldr R. Burns, with Fg. Off. W. Smith as his gunner, took-off in Defiant T4008 on patrol but their radio failed whilst over Wales and they soon became lost. Unable to find a safe way down through the clouds and with severe fuel shortage they baled out shortly before 01:40 hours. The pilot landed safety about 4 miles south of Llangurig and the gunner at Dolfor, near Newtown, breaking his ankle on uneven ground. The aircraft crashed on the hillside at Graig Safn-y-Coed near Rhayader.

Later, unaware of the fate of the two crew members, 96 squadron organised a search. Consequently, Flt Lt Verity DFC with Sgt Armstrong took-off in another Defiant★, while Sgt Scott with an unnamed corporal took-off in a third. Soon, Verity's engine began to overheat and with his gunner, he baled out, landing not far from Fg. Off. Smith, near Newtown!

When Sgt Scott in the third Defiant struck trouble, he ordered the corporal to bale out, but discovered that his passenger had not been instructed in the use of the parachute! Scott decided to attempt a forced landing and indeed would have accomplished this successfully were it not for a common Defiant undercarriage fault which caused the starboard leg to collapse; nevertheless the crew were uninjured.

★ ★ ★

I spoke to a farmer who lived nearby and he directed me to the site; only a metal detector reveals anything now, although I was told that a large piece of structure was discovered in the woods below the crash site not too many years ago. Eventually, however, I did come across a small piece of spar, still bearing original paint. Attached to it was a small, broken alloy casting stamped with the manufacturer's name "Birmal". I had heard of this firm and, finding their number from Directory Enquiries, got their address and wrote to them. A reply, bearing a different company's letterhead informed me that the firm had closed down the week before I had written and no information was available.

Of course, there is no sign of where Sgt Farmer's aircraft came down as it was recovered virtually intact. I was, however, keen to find where Flt Lt Verity's N1595 crashed. (Flt Lt V.B.S. Verity, a New Zealander, was awarded the DFC whilst flying Hurricanes with 229 squadron, at Northolt, during the Battle of Britain).

In the hope that someone might remember the incident, but without a map reference, I began the laborious task of contacting farmers in the vicinity of the crash site of Halifax DG358 (page 90) as I had heard that the Defiant had come down somewhere near Newtown.

★ N1595

Eventually I was directed to Mrs Thomas, the farmer's wife at Bryn farm during the war and she told me about the events of that November morning:

Mrs Thomas was preparing an early breakfast for her two sons when they heard the sound of an aeroplane approaching. Going to the window, she saw an aircraft coming from the east. Two figures fell away from it and descended by parachute. The aircraft fell sharply, crashing about 100 yards from the house and exploded. The shock was so great that even today, over 50 years after the event, Mrs Thomas is still nervous when a low-flying aircraft comes over.

Troops were sent in to guard the remains (without a guard, local children would soon have run off with most of the wreckage). A "Queen Mary" trailer, over 50 feet long, was sent to take the debris away but, because of its size, could get no nearer than Pantycrai School. Here it was parked for a week, whilst smaller vehicles ferried the remains from Bryn farm.

There is an indentation in the field adjacent to the farmhouse where the Defiant crashed. With permission from Roy Richards who grazes the land now, I searched the field, finding a couple of alloy pieces bearing the Boulton and Paul inspector's stamps.

Boulton-Paul Defiant
in night camouflage.

Southern ridge of Graig-safn-y-coed
T4008 crashed just to the right
of the gully that can be seen in
the centre of the picture.

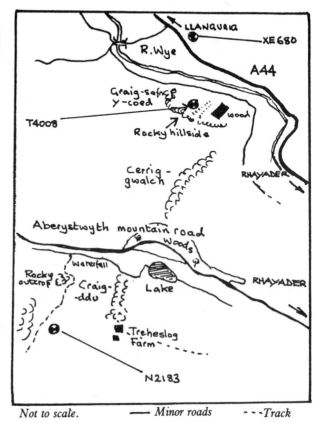

Not to scale.　　——— *Minor roads*　　- - -*Track*

The 4 gun turret which was the Defiant's sole armament. It is shown here with guns pointing forwards, a position which a mechanism prevented their firing for reasons which are readily apparent.

The farmer also told me of a crash he had witnessed some 20 years earlier, when a low-flying aircraft had circled in bad weather, as though trying to fix his position. It turned sharply and crashed into a field alongside the A44 trunk road. He and another farmer had found the pilot dead in his ejector seat near the road.

This turned out to be Hunter XE680 of 738 squadron Fleet Air Arm which crashed on March 3rd, 1969. I went to the nearest farm to the position and the farmer told me where to look but, despite a thorough search, no sign of the tragedy was found.

MR T4008
136/937724

MR N1595
136/071001

MR XE680
136/929738

Crash site of N1595 in foreground, showing proximity to farmhouse.

Vickers-Armstrong's Wellington Mk 1C BJ601

April 11th, 1944 was a typical spring day at Wern Breig farm. Mrs Pugh, the farmer's wife busied herself in the kitchen, while, two fields away, her husband was ploughing, using two horses; easier to keep during the war than a tractor.

Next to the window, the sheep grazed peacefully in the lush grass; overhead, the distant drone of an aircraft could be heard.

Earlier that day, at 22 OTU Wellesbourne Mountford, near Stratford-upon-Avon, Wellington BJ601 had taken off on a training exercise over Wales. During the flight, an engine failed, and the pilot tried to feather the propeller, but without success. (After an engine failure the propeller blades must be aligned with the direction of flight, otherwise continued rotation can cause the engine to break up. More importantly, they can cause an unacceptable level of drag which can reduce flying speed.)

After several attempts at feathering, the aircraft was abandoned; the crew parachuting to safety. With no guiding hand at the controls, the aircraft descended, and crashed into the field next to Wern Breig farmhouse. Mrs Pugh remembers it whooshing overhead before exploding; Mr Pugh left his ploughing, and ran across to see if there were any survivors. The only casualties were some sheep which were set on fire by the blazing fuel, and for which Mr Pugh later received compensation from the Air Ministry.

A crash crew came from somewhere in the Midlands and spent a couple of weeks clearing up. Mrs Pugh often gave them eggs to take home at weekends; a valuable commodity in those days. Mr Pugh has since passed away, but Mrs Pugh lives happily in nearby Rhayader.

As the site is flat agricultural land, the chances of finding the exact spot, let alone any wreckage, were remote. However, by sheer good luck, a farmer, who turned out to be the present owner, was seen feeding the sheep, and on making enquiries, he told me that my map reference was quite a bit out, and he directed me to the right field, and gave me permission to search. He told me that a couple of years earlier, someone had found a bomb fin. He said that there were two indentations in the grass where the engines had been. He must have known his land like the back of his hand; I couldn't see any indentations!

I spent an hour with the metal detector, combing the ground, and was about to give up when I detected a large object. On digging it up, it turned out to be a mud-encrusted, very badly corroded, aluminium object, quite heavy. On cleaning this, most of the aluminium crumbled away revealing a beautifully preserved bomb release mechanism. It was only prevented from actually working by the operating cable which had rusted up inside it.

MR 147/992639

An OTU Wellington turns onto course after take-off.

Wern Breig farm.
BJ601 crashed in the field in the
foreground.   The   hills   in   the
background are Y Gamriw where
Avro Anson N5019 crashed in 1940.
No sign of this remains.

Part of the bomb release mechanism
of BJ601.

Boeing B17F Flying Fortress 42-5906

Although the first units of the 8th Army Air Force arrived in Britain in July 1942, the early raids were really a matter of training for what was to come. It was not until January 1943 that Germany itself was attacked.

However, on September 16th, 1943, the aircraft factory and airfield at Bordeaux was to be the target for a force of B17s from the 388th and 390th Bomb Groups. B17F 42-5906 of the 567 Bomb Squadron piloted by Lt H. Cox and named 'Sondra Kay' after the baby of one of the crew members, left its base at Knettishall, Suffolk as one of 16 from that squadron.

However, cloud over the target prevented bombing and the aircraft proceeded to the secondary target which was the submarine pens at La Pallice. On the return flight the formations ran into rain and low cloud and aircraft were unable to stay in formation and returned independently. In darkness and rain, one crashed in the Black Mountains, another on Exmoor and another made a forced landing on three engines at Shobden. 'Sondra Kay' crossed the coast at 20:37 hours and some time later and with fuel running short and in poor visibility crashed into Rhiw-gwraidd at Upper Cilgu near Rhayader. The crew of 10 were all killed.

★ ★ ★

Boeing B-17F

*Upper Cilgu farm
42-5906 crashed in this field.*

The crew of 'Sondra Kay' photographed just a few weeks before the tragedy.
Photo: USAF via E. Doylerush

Turning off the A470, the drive of two miles or so, is up an ever steepening road with stunning views of the surrounding countryside. The farmer at Upper Cilgu farm, the nearest habitation to the site, allows me to search the field. This site has been looked at many times before so expectations of finding anything of importance is low, but the tiniest fragment will at least confirm the place where the crash took place which, after all, is the object of the exercise. In the event, up near the highest hedge many small items are seen; the name plate from a generator, some odd pieces of structure and a few unfired 0.5″ cartridge cases.

A few hundred yards away a TV mast has been erected and it is hard to pass that way without being reminded of the tragic events of that day nearly fifty years ago.

An odd sequel to this visit was found in an antique shop in nearby Rhayader, where a highly polished round of 0.5″ ammunition was on display. On its base it had the same markings as those found on site. It had been fired, but a bullet had been replaced in the case. Did it come, at some time, from the same aircraft? Who knows.

MR 147/014632

Avro Lancaster B Mk III JB471

The Pathfinder Force was set up by a youthful Australian Air Commodore, Don Bennett, at the instigation of the Air Staff, because of the inability of Bomber Command to bomb with any real accuracy. Initially, the PFF used the most experienced crews in the Command and was responsible for marking the targets with ground and air markers for the Main Force aircraft.

It was not, however, universally welcomed; A.M. Harris himself disliking the idea of some sort of elite force within the Command. Despite this, it went from strength to strength, one of its most famous exponents being John Searby DSO, DFC, leader of the attack on the German experimental establishment at Peenemunde, where the German flying bombs and rockets were being developed.

★ ★ ★

On April 11th, 1944, JB471 of the Pathfinder Force Navigation Training Unit Warboys took off on a training flight which passed over Wales. The two pilots were Wing Commander J. Green and Flt Lt J. Soper. During the flight the aircraft went into a steep dive and at 4000 feet at high speed, the tail became detached due to the excessive strain on the elevators in attempting to pull out; the forward fuselage also broke away. The aircraft crashed and burnt out; there were no survivors from the crew of eight.

JB471 was delivered to the RAF on October 18th, 1943 and flew with 156 Squadron before being allocated to the PFF NTU. It had flown a total of 272 hours.

★ ★ ★

A Lancaster taxies into dispersal.

Boggy ground at Cefn Gast farm where JB471 crashed. Much small wreckage must remain here despite proximity of main road.

When looking for the site of Wellington R1597 I met Mr Price of Troedyrhiw Fach farm who, after telling me about the "Wimpey" also told me a Lancaster had also crashed nearby in 1944. As I had no knowledge of this occurrence, I decided to look into it. Mr Price told me that the aircraft had crashed into boggy ground at Cefn Gast farm, close to a minor road and, when he went over to see it immediately following the accident, he found a crew member up to his chest in the bog. At first sight he thought the man was still alive but, unfortunately, he was dead.

The farm is now owned by the son of the war-time owner, Mr Evans, who was very helpful in pointing out where various parts fell. This was mostly in the bog, so I was, because of a recent drought, able to look over the whole area. Unfortunately, owing to the roughness of the terrain and clumps of bog grass, I was unable to bring any fragments to light, but doubtless, the bog contains many secrets.

MR 147/905469

Miles Master III W8773 and DL570

The Master was a two-seat advanced trainer, rather similar to the well-known 'Harvard', an American aircraft also used in great numbers by the RAF for pilot training. Powered by a 825 hp Pratt and Whitney Wasp Junior radial engine it could attain a speed of 232 mph and had a service ceiling of 27,300 feet.

It was used by (Pilots') Advanced Flying Units and was usually the last aircraft the pilots flew before moving on to the OTUs for the specific fighter aircraft they were to fly in action. (These had no provision for an instructor.) Six hundred of the Mark III version were built before production ceased in 1942.

★ ★ ★

No. 5 (P) AFU was based at High Ercall in Shropshire, when, on October 4th, 1942, two aircraft took off together for a cross-country formation exercise. On the left, it is believed, in W8773, was Sgt T. Hyndman with his instructor P/O J. Chinnery, whilst in the other aircraft was Sgt R. Camsburn, a Canadian, with Sgt H.B. Hubbard as the instructor.

After flying for about 1 hour 20 minutes and with the ground covered by thick cloud, P/O Chinnery (W8773) who was doing the navigation for the both aircraft, decided that they must have crossed the Welsh coast and began his descent, followed by Sgt Hubbard in the other aircraft. They had, in fact, some 25 miles still to go and P/O Chinnery on the left, emerging first through the gloom, was confronted by a high rocky outcrop on moorland at Abergwesyn, north of Llanwrtyd Wells. After striking the ground, the aircraft caught fire, was partially burnt out and both crew members were killed.

Almost instantaneously, a little above and to the right, Sgt Hubbard, in DL570, also came down through the cloud. The sight that met his eyes caused both dismay and relief. Relief, for although he could see the burning wreckage of the other aircraft, ahead of him was a plateau sloping down to the Afon Gwesyn, which might be his salvation. Although the aircraft was travelling at high speed, it hit the ground at a shallow angle and turned over onto its back. Neither of the occupants was injured.

★ ★ ★

The Abergwesyn Mountain road from Beulah to Tregaron makes a splendid outing through forest and high moorland, with buzzards and sometimes red kites wheeling overhead. About 5 miles from Beulah, behind Ty Mawr, a farmhouse on the right, there is a footpath which follows the river valley. In about a mile or so, a tree-lined stream can be seen coming down from the right; the site is just a few yards beyond it on the opposite side of the river. If you come to a second small waterfall, although a pleasant place for a picnic, you have gone too far!

Much wreckage is to be found: electrical panels, engine cowlings and much skinning, some still bearing the yellow paint with which the underside of the aircraft was painted. (The upper surfaces were in standard camouflage finish.) The most prominent piece to be seen is the central frame of the cockpit canopy, the camouflaged skinning attached to it singed by the fire. It is difficult to be sure to which aircraft the wreckage belongs, as it has been moved, in the main, to one spot. However, as DL570 did not catch fire after turning over, it is most likely that it was recovered virtually intact. The remains therefore would appear to be from P/O Chinnery's W8773.

MR 147/858556

Miles Master III

Left: Wreckage of W8773 above Abergwesyn. The plateau below is the most likely crash site of DL570 flown by Sgt Hubbard who, with his pupil, survived the crash.

Right: Centre frame of cockpit canopy.

Vickers-Armstrong's Wellington T Mk X PG312

Long after the war the Wellington soldiered on as a navigational trainer, eventually being replaced by the Valetta and Varsity from the same stable.

On November 5th, 1951 PG312 of the No. 1 Air Navigation School took off from Hullavington, Wilts, on an exercise to Merlin Head Scotland, and Carlisle. The captain was Sqn Ldr P.M. Procter and the trainee navigators Cadets G. Johnson and A. Good. On their return to Hullavington, bad weather prevented a landing and the aircraft was diverted to Valley on Anglesey. At 22:45 hrs the starboard engine stopped and the captain ordered the crew to don parachutes. Four minutes later, the port engine also stopped and the pilot ordered the crew to abandon the aircraft. There was insufficient time for the pilot to parachute to safety and he was killed when the aircraft crashed at Fronfelin farm at Old Hall. The surviving crew were taken to Llanidloes Hospital where the wireless operator was found to be suffering from shock.

The aircraft had been airborne for 5 hours 50 minutes and fuel starvation, possibly caused by incorrect selection of fuel cocks could have been the reason for the engine failures.

★ ★ ★

PG312 crashed into the banks of the Avon just below the copse of trees at left centre of the photograph.

A Mark X Wellington similar to PG312 although the latter was finished in silver. Note the fairing which replaces the front gun turret.

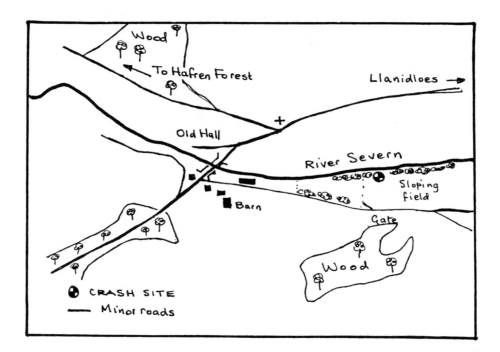

On going to the site, nothing was found, though an enquiry of a young farm hand elicited the information that, although it was before he was born, he was told that quite a few years previously a wheel and oleo leg had been uncovered whilst ploughing and they were both in excellent condition, with gleaming metal and air in the tyre.

The only thing to have been brought to light recently was a rusty piece of metal he pointed out standing on the farmyard wall. This turned out to be a sleeve from a Bristol Hercules engine.

With his permission I used my metal detector over the field and on the river bank discovered a badly corroded piece of aircraft skinning; nothing further was found. As the crash occurred on the river bank the scouring effect of the fast flowing waters has probably swept away much material over the intervening years.

The farm hand took me over to see his grandmother living nearby in the hope that she could tell me more. Mrs Jane Evans told me that she remembered it well; it was bonfire night and her husband was riding his bicycle home when it happened. Although this was interesting, I was more intrigued when she told me about the pre-war crash of the Fairey Battle, the location of which had so far eluded me.

MR 136/915846

Evasive Action: Handley-Page Halifax BIII LW366

The Mark III version of the Halifax was powered by four Bristol Hercules XVI radial engines of 1615 hp each which increased its maximum speed by nearly 20 mph which in turn greatly increased its rate of survival over enemy territory. Because of their relatively poor performance, earlier marks of the Halifax had, by the end of 1943, been restricted to less heavily defended targets; with the introduction of the Mark III this restriction was lifted.

Now Halifax crews had a "Shining Sword"* equal to the Lancaster.

LW366, a Mark III, was built by English Electric at their Preston works and was allocated to 420 Squadron on December 16th, 1943.

Such were the numbers of Canadian airmen within Bomber Command that an all-Canadian group, No. 6, was set up equipped in the main with the Halifax and 420 Squadron belonged to this group.

★ ★ ★

Harry Skeet Hardy was born on November 7th, 1912 in Toronto, Canada. He married in April 1941 and on January 30th, 1942, when he was nearly 30 years old, he enlisted in the RCAF for the "Duration of the Emergency", a title also given to conscripts on this side of the Atlantic. He went to aircrew Initial Training School, where physical training and drill was the order of the day in July of 1942 and, two months later, as a Temporary Sergeant, commenced pilot training, being awarded his flying badge on April 15th, 1943.

On the 30th of the month he went on Embarkation Leave and, on May 27th embarked on a troopship at Halifax for Europe. (A rather apt departure point, as most Canadian airmen were destined to fly the Halifax bomber.)

Arriving in the UK some 9 days later, there followed a spell at No. 15 Pilot's Advanced Flying Unit after which he was posted to No. 22 OTU Wellesbourne Mountford near Stratford-on-Avon where he was joined by the others who were to form his crew. During the next three months they completed nearly 100 hours flying in the Wellington III before leaving for 1659 HCU where, with two additional crew members, they flew the Halifax Mark II and V finally moving to 420 Squadron. They were now ready for operations, with 73 flying hours on the Halifax to their credit; the crew consisted:

F.S.	HARDY	Pilot
Sgt	CUNNINGS	Bomb Aimer
Fg. Off.	HEDRICH	Navigator
Fg. Off.	JAMES	WOP/AG
Sgt	NIXON	Mid-Upper Gunner
Sgt	JOHNSON	Rear Gunner
Sgt	WILLOUGHBY	Flight Engineer

★ ★ ★

The weather at Tholthorpe, near York on February 29th, 1944 was hazy with a watery winter sun lighting the airfield, with just 3/10th cloud at 2,000 feet. Skeet Hardy and his crew took-off at 1340 for a cross-country flight and by 1500 hours were over Wales at 20,000 feet where they were to practice evasive action. (With the relatively poor armament of RAF Heavy Bombers the main defence against night fighters was "evasive action", normally a corkscrew like, sickening motion which enemy pilots found hard to follow.) The manoeuvre commenced with a sharp descent, but when the pilot hauled back the control column to pull out, the controls became sloppy and the aircraft, now climbing almost vertically, could not be controlled. It lost airspeed almost immediately and with a violent flip, stalled and went into a

* Air Chief Marshal Harris called the Lancaster " . . . a Shining Sword put into the hands of Bomber Command crews."

spin. The pilot tried all he could to recover but the aircraft then went into a "falling leaf" condition. The Bomb Aimer and Navigator, without their parachutes were thrown through the perspex nose and were killed. The Engineer's parachute burst open inside the aircraft and was sucked out through the hole in the nose dragging the hapless Sgt Willoughby out behind it knocking him out in the process, but he recovered during his descent and landed safely apart from slight injuries. (Sgt D. Willoughby was later commissioned, promoted to Fg. Officer and was awarded the D.F.C. He died in Australia in 1965.)

A Halifax BIII of 77 squadron.

LW366 crashed in this field.

*Handley-Page Halifax LW385,
a close relative. Identification
of Halifax mark and series numbers
is a job for the expert!*

Right: Hafod Fawr farm, near Cross Inn.
The crashing aircraft narrowly missed the house, ending up in the field beyond the trees, which were considerably smaller 50 years ago!

F. Sgt Harry S. Hardy

The farmhouse, with, on the left, the remaining wall of the barn destroyed by the crashing aircraft.

The Wireless Operator managed to get out of the escape hatch at low altitude and also survived the ordeal. The aircraft struck the ground at Hafod Fawr farm at Cross Inn near Aberaeron in a port slipping turn with great violence, one wing scything off the roof of a barn setting fire to the hay inside and a propeller flew off across the farmyard. The aircraft narrowly missed the farmhouse and crashed in a field 300 yards away and burnt out.

Some burned parachute cords were found caught up in the elevators as if a third crew member had tried to escape, presumably the rear gunner.

Later investigation of the wreckage showed that the most likely cause of the accident was that the elevator controls had broken. The Investigating Officer recommended that all Halifax control rods be checked, but the AOC thought that as present checks were very stringent and as no specific point of failure could be established, no purpose could be served by this.

*F. Sgt Hardy is buried in
Chester Military Cemetery.*

*1993: The watch tower at former
R.A.F. Tholthorpe.*

*A Halifax Bill of 420 squadron
RCAF prepares to take-off from its
base at Tholthorpe near York.*

A potent reason for Evasive Action.*
Left to Right:
1. *0.303" cartridge as used by
   Bomber Command throughout the
   war.*
2. *0.5" bullet as used by USAAF.*
3. *20mm cannon shell similar to that
   used by German night fighters.
   (It took an average of 50 rounds to
   bring down a 4 engined bomber.)*

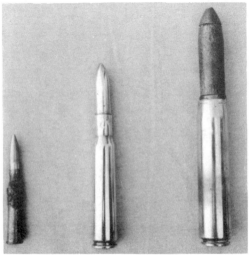

** For more technically minded
readers it has to be stated that
the lack of ventral armament
on RAF bombers was probably
more important than the calibre
of the guns.*

At the time of the crash LW366 had completed 80 and a half hours flying time in its two months RAF service. Flight Sergeant Hardy and his crew are buried in the Commonwealth War Graves Section at Blacon Cemetery, Chester.

★ ★ ★

At flat field, easily accessible sites, there can be little expectation of finding any wreckage, but unlike some mountain locations, what can often be found is a personal story of someone living there at the time. It took me quite some time making enquiries in the area until I discovered that the keeper of the village Post Office lived there as a teenager during the war. (I had been told by one couple that there was a memorial to the crash in the nearby hills, but the "memorial" turned out to be an Ordnance Survey mapping point).

The postmaster remembered the incident well and soon I was speaking to Mrs Davies who still lives next door to Hafod Fawr. "This vast black shape came out of the sky," she said, so much bigger than she had expected any aeroplane to be, few country people having seen an aeroplane at close quarters. She remembers the hay in the barn on fire and the propeller nearby. The locations of the hay barn, house and field show that the crashing aircraft missed the house by the narrowest of margins.

Mrs Davies recalls the horror of finding the top of a skull, with red hair, in a corner of the field. Her father found an arm in an RAF sleeve, with a gold ring on a finger of the hand, just outside the farm gate.

As with most tragedies, however horrible, Mrs Davies told me that there was much excitement amongst the village youngsters, to whom the war must have seemed a long way off.

The field where the aircraft crashed is very boggy and many fragments must have sunk deep into the wet ground, the movement of cattle helping in this process. Nevertheless, I discovered dozens of small pieces, a couple with serial numbers identifying them as Halifax parts and with inspector's stamps for English Electric at Preston, thus establishing the exact location of the crash. From this I was able to deduce that if it was indeed a wing which hit the barn roof then it is most likely that it had become separated from the fuselage prior to the aircraft hitting the ground. The aircraft most likely passed the northern side of the farmhouse pieces falling from its starboard side onto the farmyard and barn.

Of course, it is often just too late arriving at places like this. Mrs Davies told me that, when demolishing an outbuilding the previous year, she had found some remains of the crash including a pile of leaflets in German, which were all consigned to the builders skip!

She also told me of a memorial stone in the hills near Lledrod. I decided to investigate this and, in misty rain and low cloud, probably similar conditions to the day of the crash, found the stone on a hill near Trefenter. It turned out to be of recent origin, being the site of the crash of Phantom ZE358 of 74 Squadron which occurred on August 26th, 1987.

LW366	ZE358
MR 146/552641	MR 135/611682

Plaque at site of crash of Phantom ZE358

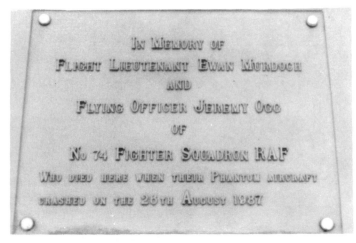

Hawker Henley L3435

First flying in 1937, the Henley was designed as a fast light bomber but there were already doubts regarding the chances of survival in combat of the Fairey Battle and the Henley's 30 mph speed advantage was not thought sufficient for it to be much of an improvement. It was powered by a Rolls-Royce 'Merlin' engine of 1030 hp and could attain a maximum speed of 272 mph, with internal stowage for a 750 lb bomb load. It carried a crew of 2.

With 200 aircraft in service, or in course of construction other duties had to found for the Henley. As the target towing aircraft at that time were elderly biplanes, it was decided to convert the Henleys into target tugs. To wind in the drogue targets a winch was fitted, powered by a slip-stream driven propeller on the port side of the aircraft.

At first the Henleys were used by Air Gunnery Schools for air-to-air firing but soon the wear and tear on the engines was such that they had to be limited to 220 mph, a speed too low for the job in hand. They were then re-assigned to Anti-Aircraft Co-operation Units, which had a number of independent flights, usually near gunnery schools. However, the bigger drogue targets needed for AA practice produced even more drag and thus more engine wear. So, of the 200 Henleys built, over 50 were written off because of engine failures.

No. 1605 Flight was based at Tywyn airfield, a small grass strip just north of the town on the banks of the Dysynni river. (Today, the buildings are used by the Army as a Climbing School.) The Royal Artillery unit they served was a Tonfannau, just 2 miles north of the airfield, which, apart from a couple of buildings and a dilapidated railway station, no longer exists.

It is difficult to imagine, on visiting this peaceful area today, that there were at least seven engine-related crashes at or near Tywyn.

One of these involved Fg. Off. A.H. Rawson, a World War I pilot and civil test pilot. After take-off from Tywyn Airfield he encountered engine problems and decided to return to base. On the approach, however, his engine lost power, the aircraft stalled and crashed half a mile north of the airfield. Both Rawson and his crew, A/C Sharp, lost their lives in the resulting fire.

★ ★ ★

On May 5th, 1942, Sgt H. Wilson, with Aircraftsman A. Williams as winch operator, took-off from Tywyn in Henley L3435 on a target towing sortie. Minutes later, at 0912 hours, due either to loss of power or misjudgement, the aircraft stalled in a turn and crashed into the sea 50 feet below the low tide mark, breaking up. A/C Williams escaped with a fractured femur and went to get help to release the pilot who was trapped in the wreckage. However, by the time help arrived the tide had come in, covering the aircraft and drowning the pilot. His body was recovered later that evening when the tide had retreated. Sgt Wilson (RNZAF), aged 24, was buried in Tywyn Cemetery, only two and a half miles from where he died. Army personnel helped in the recovery of the airframe but when it came to the engine they seem to have lost heart and decided that it was not worth winching it up the cliff or dragging it the half mile or so across the rocky foreshore to the nearest road. So it was left and there it remains today.

★ ★ ★

The beach at Tonfannau is a mass of jumbled rocks and boulders of unusual shapes and sizes, some worn by the sea into sharp-edged designs that would fit into any gallery of modern sculpture. It is approached by a small road which leads directly down to the beach, from Caedu farm, near Rhoslefain. The engine lies about half a mile to the south, just before reaching Owain's cave. (So named after Owain Glyndŵr, the Welsh National hero, its high vaulted roof a magnet for local adventure groups who use it for climbing and abseiling). The tide here comes in rapidly and in my mind's eye I could see it engulfing the aircraft.

Because of the movement of the sand, the engine is often completely covered, so it is a matter of luck as to whether it can be found. It was sand covered on my last visit but the beauty of the place made me stay. Whilst idly poking about in nearby rock pools, I found a fragment of alloy with many securing bolts, which later turned out to be part of the 'Merlin' supercharger housing. But beware, the shore here is littered with alloy, fragments coming from wrecked boats and even aluminium roof panels torn off in gales. There are no airframe parts remaining.

There is another fly in the ointment; this beautiful Tonfannau beach claimed two other aircraft.

Previously, on October 29th, 1940, Sgt Thomas had a propeller fault on L3312 and crash landed here. (It is on record that the engine from this aircraft was dragged along the beach a week later.) On February 4th, 1943, P/O Brolyn, in L3297, had an engine failure on take-off and crashed, virtually on the same spot.

So, which engine lies under the sand? As the serial number is no longer discernible all that can really be said is that it is certainly from a Hawker Henley and that will have to do.

MR 135/564055

Tonfannau beach..
L3435 was dragged up to this point,
but the sand shown in the foreground,
often shifts after gales covering the
remains of the engine.

Another piece of wreckage
from Tonfannau beach, though this
is of recent origin. It is part of
a pilotless drone launched from
nearby Llanbedr.

Fragment of supercharger housing of
Rolls-Royce Merlin XX engine.

The New Zealand pilot of Henley
L3435 rests in Tywyn Cemetery.

Republic P47 Thunderbolt 42-75101

The Thunderbolt was one of the foremost American fighters of World War II. Powered by a Pratt and Whitney Double Wasp radial engine, of 2300 hp, it could attain a speed of 427 mph. With a range of nearly 2000 miles, when using external tanks, it escorted the bombers of the 8th Air Force deep into Nazi Germany. Later it was also used for ground attack and its heavy construction, like that of its RAF counterpart the Typhoon, made it extremely effective in that role. Over 15,000 Thunderbolts had been manufactured by the end of the war.

★ ★ ★

The scene which greeted American airmen on arrival in the UK must have been, to say the least, somewhat of a culture shock. Being housed in corrugated "Nissen" huts (nothing to do with the motor manufacturer!) with indifferent food (by US standards) and on camps which were often deep in mud, must have brought home to them the conditions under which British airmen, and the other Services for that matter, had been living for the previous 3 years. Nowhere more was the shock felt than when it came to actual flying. Trained in sunny areas of the US, with little bad weather and few natural hazards, it took a period of adjustment before most were fit to go into action.

The 485th Fighter Training Group based at Atcham near Shrewsbury had the task, among other things, of familiarising pilots with European conditions.

On May 4th, 1944, Lt Barrett took off on a low-level training flight over Wales. It appears that he entered cloud and struck the hillside at Mynydd Copog near Mallwyd, where he was killed.

★ ★ ★

Since then a forest has been planted but only to the edge of the crash site, and some wreckage has been moved in the process. However, this is an easily accessible site (with the landowners permission) and is very satisfying in that a vast amount of wreckage remains. Metal skinning with dark olive paint is there in profusion, as are stainless steel items from the area of the turbo-charger. The main item of interest must be the Pratt and Whitney engine, which although badly corroded, still remains.

I suppose that, although on relatively low ground, the reason for the large amount of wreckage must be that the site is well away from public footpaths and holiday areas.

MR 125/884144

Above: Republic P47D
Thunderbolt at low level.

Above: Pratt and Whitney 'Double
Wasp' R-2800-59, 2,300 hp.

Right: General view of crash site.

Handley-Page Halifax BV DG358

The Halifax was produced, not only by Handley-Page at their Radlett works but by over 40 factories with hundreds of sub-contractors.

Rootes Securities were awarded contracts for over a thousand Halifaxes, of various marks, for production at their factory at Speke near Liverpool; contract no. B637/C4 being for a batch of 150 mainly Mark V aircraft.

DG358 left the factory early in 1943 and went directly to an HCU, without being used on operations and, in November of that year, was allotted to 1667 HCU at Faldingworth, not far from Lincoln.

★ ★ ★

On the morning of January 23rd, 1944, DG358, coded "J", took-off on a training flight with Sgt P.K. Bennett at the controls and a crew of 8. They were flying at 20,000 feet over Welsh border country when the starboard outer engine (Merlin XX serial no. 393891) failed. It proved impossible to maintain height on the remaining three engines, so Sgt Bennett began a descent into thick storm clouds, possibly Cumulo-Nimbus. Ice began to build up and violent air currents tore the airframe apart, the starboard wing shearing off and smashing the tail unit on the same side.

*A Halifax B Mk V. being serviced in
a typical wartime environment.*

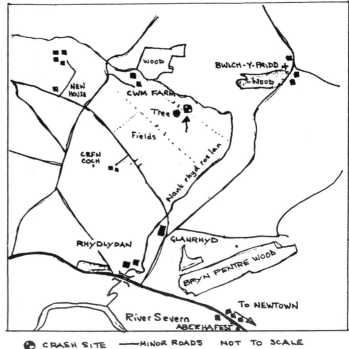

CRASH SITE ──── MINOR ROADS   NOT TO SCALE

The aircraft crashed into fields near Bryn-y-groes at 1440 hours. There were no survivors from the nine on board.

As the aircraft had only flown a total of 78 hours up to the time of the disaster, it may well have had a history of unserviceability; the very low total hours flown equates to only about 7 hours per month throughout its service.

★ ★ ★

Contacting Michael Jones at Cwm farm proved most interesting, as the aircraft crashed only half a mile from the farmhouse and his father took him down to the site at the time. Wreckage was strewn for hundreds of yards down the meadow, to the banks of Nant-rhyd-ros-lan. In heavy rain the bodies of the crew were collected and Mr Jones' neighbour provided a tractor and trailer to take them to nearby Bwlch-y-Ffridd, where they laid in the village Institute. A detachment of the local Home-Guard mounted a guard on the wreckage until an RAF salvage team arrived to remove the debris, a task which took nearly three weeks. Their "Queen Mary" low-loaders had to travel some distance across the muddy fields from the nearest road.

★ ★ ★

Mr Jones' son took me bouncing over the fields on his Honda "quad", leaving me to spend a few hours trying to envisage the scene and perhaps unearth a few fragments to positively identify the site. I learned that the original meadow has been divided by a fence since the war.

All larger parts have gone (some to Cosford Aerospace Museum quite recently) but small pieces, bearing the "57" prefix, can still be found scattered around the muddy fields.

MR 136/058948

DG358 crashed towards the camera,
narrowly missing the large tree. The
hedge did not exist at that time.

De Havilland Mosquito PR Mk 9 LR412

Photographic Reconnaissance was an essential part of the Allied air offensive against the Axis powers. Photographing enemy targets both before and after attacks showed the extent of the damage and whether more action would be needed. The whereabouts of the German pocket battleships, which presented a constant threat to Allied shipping, had to be monitored and it was a Mosquito of 540 squadron which first photographed the German VI flying bombs at the research centre at Peenamunde.

The PR squadrons were mainly based at Benson in Oxfordshire, though there were squadrons in the Middle and Far east. When it is considered that a sortie to Berlin or Poland entailed a thousand mile flight over enemy territory, mostly in daylight, in an unarmed aircraft then the bravery of these airmen, many of whom lost their lives, can be appreciated.

★ ★ ★

The Mosquito PR Mark 9 was powered by two Rolls-Royce "Merlin" 72 engines of 1680 hp each. It had a top speed of over 415 mph, a range of over 1400 miles and carried a crew of 2. A total of 90 aircraft of this mark were built.

LR412 was one of a batch of 41 aircraft built at the De Havilland works at Hatfield, Herts. and had, up to April 9th, 1944, a very successful record of operations. Official records show that it flew the following sorties:

JUNE 18th, 1943	TURIN and MILAN
AUGUST 11th, 1943	NUREMBURG (After an attack by 653 Bomber Command aircraft)
AUGUST 15th, 1943	MILAN (After an attack by 140 Lancasters)
AUGUST 17th, 1943	CHEMNITZ and LEIPZIG
AUGUST 18th, 1943	TURIN, MILAN and DIJON
SEPTEMBER 6th, 1943	MUNICH and STUTTGART (After an attack by 404 aircraft)
SEPTEMBER 20th, 1943	CANNES
SEPTEMBER 30th, 1943	BOCHUM (After an attack by 352 aircraft)
OCTOBER 3rd, 1943	MUNICH (After an attack by 294 aircraft)
OCTOBER 17th, 1943	MAGDEBURG
NOVEMBER 8th, 1943	KNABEN and RJUKAN
NOVEMBER 28th, 1943	TRONDHEIM (Possibly looking for battleship 'Tirpitz'
DECEMBER 13th, 1943	NORTHERN FRANCE and PARIS
JANUARY 4th, 1944	BERLIN (After an attack by 383 aircraft)
JANUARY 7th, 1944	POSNAN

Note: In the attacks mentioned above a total of 77 Bomber Command aircraft were lost.

LR412 Photographed not long before its loss on February 9th, 1944.

Erosion of the propeller blades caused by the initial fire and subsequent weathering.

The crash site of LR412 on Arun Fawddwy. The object in front of the propeller is an oil tank.

On February 9th, 1944, Mosquito LR412 with Fg. Off. Narek Slonski (Polish) as pilot and Fg. Off. Paul Riches DFC as navigator, took off from Benson on an airtest to check flap operation and on a cross-country exercise. It appears that they crossed the Welsh coast, possibly passing overhead Llanbedr airfield, travelling in an easterly direction. With such an experienced navigator, the reason why they were flying at such a low altitude over mountainous country is a matter of conjecture, however, a wrong altimeter setting cannot be ruled out. LR412 struck the 2450 foot ridge near Drws Bach on Arun Fawddwy. At this point, some 500 feet below the summit and some distance to the south of it, a little extra altitude would have saved them. The aircraft struck the ground and exploded, killing both crew members instantly.

Although the aircraft was reported overdue at 1200 that day, at Benson, it was another 5 days before the aircraft was found.

★ ★ ★

The walk to this site is a very pleasant one for hill-walkers whether or not they are interested in crash sites and, if about 5 hours is allowed, there will be plenty of time for a leisurely picnic. The start is made at Esgair Gawr farm (the Outdoor Leisure Map No. 23 is better for walkers in this area) MR 816224. If arriving by car, do not forget to ask permission of the farmer, Mr R. Roberts, before you leave it, as the footpath goes through his land.

Go through the farmyard and follow the path, alongside a stone wall. After crossing a forestry road the path is ill-defined but goes between two areas of forestry. When that on the left finishes, you will find, a few yards further on, on the right, a deep ravine with a stream rushing along its rock strewn bottom. Look across a little to the left of the end of the wood and a white topped post will be seen. Walk directly to it and follow subsequent posts. At the fifth post strike off to the right at about 75° and, shortly, the next post will come into view. (Do not go straight on at the fifth post, it is very boggy.) From there onward the route is marked with white painted arrows on the rocks. On arriving at the fence on the ridge, cross the stile, turn left up the slope for about 100 yards and the site is about 50 yards to the right.

There are two gouges in the ground, probably caused by the engines, one of which is now embedded in concrete at the farm entrance. One propeller hub remains, with its blades crumbling away with corrosion. Thousands of fragments are scattered around: fuel pipes, pieces of cowling and the crew's armour plating. The main structure being of wood is not much in evidence, however, because of the force of the explosion, many small pieces of charred wood can be found up to 100 yards away in knooks and crannies in the rock. Some even have the light blue paint used on PRU aircraft still adhering to them.

If not worn out by your exertions and you have not yet eaten your lunch, retrace your steps to the stile, continue downhill for ten minutes or so. A large rocky outcrop will then be seen two hundred yards or so to the left. Walk over to it and a spectacular picnic site will be found. This walk is best done in dry weather.

MR 125 857216

The Final Journey

Having got to the last chapter of the book, the reader has by now either given up in frustration or become perhaps a bit of an enthusiast; the latter it is to be hoped.

It was never the object of this book to encourage people to rush around the countryside like demented "twitchers", trying to see how many sites they could visit or how much material they could take away. It was meant to perhaps remind people of the recent aviation history of this country and to more readily appreciate the sacrifice of those who died to keep us free, if not during the lifetime of the reader then most likely within that of his parents.

If the reader wishes to know more about the subject and this book only scratches the surface, there are a number of excellent books available, with research much deeper than that contained herein.

As the years go by, the sites become harder to find. The people who know the personal stories are leaving us and soon there will be nothing left, except for just a few aviation archaeologists who give up most of their time to research. I hope that this book will help swell the numbers of those who wish to keep these memories alive.

Finally, to keep the reader on his toes, a site that has defeated the author; perhaps you can find the exact spot? Please let me know if you do.

Vickers-Armstrong's Wellington Mk 1C N2813

On the night of May 20th, 1942 a Wellington of 18 OTU Sywell near Northampton, took-off on a cross-country flight with Sgt P. Bakalarski, a Pole, at the controls. Over Wales one engine iced up and stopped. (Only 7 months earlier another Wellington from 18 OTU, N2866, suffered the same problem and was abandoned near Llanbedr.) The aircraft began to lose height and, in deteriorating weather conditions, the pilot ordered the crew to bale out. The trainee wireless operator had failed to transmit an SOS or turn on the IFF to the No. 3 Distress Band.

The aircraft crashed at 0250 on high moorland, near Esgair Penygarreg, at about 1500 feet. It had been flying for 3 hours 10 minutes. The crew landed not far away and two were injured. The Air Officer Commanding's remarks after the accident were that as the pilot was unable to control the aircraft and in view of the terrain (sparsely populated hills), the pilot was justified in abandoning the aircraft.

(A rather obvious remark I would have thought. But then, people sitting in nice warm offices often see things differently from those sitting in a crashing aircraft, at night, in bad weather over the dark Welsh hills. Still, I suppose he had to say something.)

* * *

A Wellington bomber undergoing maintenance outside the hangar. Note the propeller in the foreground.

Tom Evans was asleep in Treheslog farm when, at about 3 a.m., there was a hammering on the front door and he opened it to find the Polish pilot on the doorstep. As the aircraft is supposed to have crashed only 10 minutes previously the pilot must have almost landed in the farmyard.

Mr Evans now lives in nearby Rhydoldog farm and remembers little else of that night 50 years ago.

The site lies on high moorland near the Rhayader-Aberystwyth mountain road. Park by a small waterfall; uninterested friends can while away a pleasant hour or two with a picnic by the stream. Nearby is a sheep pool; it is a kind of pen built right across the stream, doubtless shepherds washed the sheep here, and climb up the clearly defined track for about 25 minutes and there you are; and the best of British Luck!

Of course, my lack of success might well be attributed to the fact that, shortly after beginning the search, rain of the most vigorous Welsh kind came cascading down making it difficult to see, let alone search. But then, that is one of the pleasures of walking in Wales.

MR 147/932689

The track to Cefnrhydoldog where N2183 crashed, fortunately without loss of life.

N2183 crashed near this deserted farmhouse.

Treheslog farm where Sgt Balarski, the pilot of N2813 sought assistance in the early hours of May 21st, 1942.

Acknowledgements

The author wishes to acknowledge the help given by many people in their directions, reminiscences and photographs, of which the following is unfortunately an incomplete list.

The Bomber Command Association, Martin Bowman, The Brooklands Museum, The Canadian Defence Force, R.D. Cooling, John Davies, E. Doylerush, Brian Evans, Jane Evans, Jim Halley, A. Hipperson, The Imperial War Museum, David Jenkins, Wyn Jones, Hannah Jones, Lockheed Corporation, Roger Miles, K. Merrick, Ministry of Defence, National Archive of Canada, J. Postings, Gerald Roberts, Rolls-Royce plc., the Royal Air Force Museum, R.N.L.I., R. Read, Patrick Smith, Andrew Thomas, D.A. Wiltshire and last but by no means least, Shirley Evans who managed to put my ramblings into readable form.

Bibliography

Aircraft of the RAF since 1918, Owen Thetford, Putnam
Fallen Eagles, Eddie Doylerush, Midland Counties
The Hampden File, Harry Moyle, Air Britain
Halifax, K.A. Merrick, Aston
High Ground Wrecks, D.J. Smith, Midland Counties
No Landing Place, Eddie Doylerush, Midland Counties
Spitfire: The History, Morgan & Shacklady, Guild
Wellington: The Geodetic Giant, Martin Bowman, Airlife
Wings of War over Gwynedd, Roy Sloan, Gwasg Carreg Gwalch
"If you don't like it, you shouldn't have joined", R.A. Read (unpublished)

AVIATION IN WALES

EARLY AVIATION IN NORTH WALES by Roy Sloan

168 pages; ISBN: 0-86381-119-1; Price: £2.75

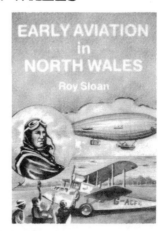

Described by the widely respected aviation historian David J. Smith as "magnificent" and an "excellent piece of work", this book sets out to chronicle the history of aviation in North Wales from the time of early nineteenth century balloon flights to the outbreak of World War II in 1939.

Well researched and illustrated with approximately sixty photographs, this book makes a notable contribution to the history of aviation in Wales.

WINGS OF WAR OVER GWYNEDD

Aviation in Gwynedd during World War II
by Roy Sloan

200 pages; many maps & illustrations; £4.50; ISBN: 0-86381-189-2

This book traces the history of aviation in Gwynedd during the momentous years of the Second World War — a period of rapid and dramatic development.

In addition to the already existing military airfield of Penrhos, seven others were established within a short period of time. Their functions ranged from providing defence cover for north west Britain, operating a Transatlantic Terminal for American aircraft, to the training of air gunners, navigators and bomb aimers.

The stories of all eight are told in detail as are those of the RAF's fighter squadrons based here, including their encounters with the Luftwaffe.

Two bombed-out aircraft manufacturers found safe haven in the county —- Saunders-Roe and Hunting Aviation — and a full account is given of their important work. There is also an overview of that perennially intriguing subject — aircarft crashes in Snowdonia.

Readable, well researched and illustrated with seventy photographs, the book provides a fascinating view of wartime aviation in Gwynedd and as such ranks as a major contribution to the history of aviation in Wales.

Aircraft Crashes
Flying accidents in Gwynedd 1910-1990
Roy Sloan

Price: £5.50; 168 pages; many photographs; ISBN: 0-86381-281-3

The sixteen stories which make up this book have been chosen in order to provide a broad view of the types of flying accidents which have taken place within the geographical boundaries of Gwynedd. The region's mountains are the highest in England and Wales and, not surprisingly, present a natural hazard themselves. In his latest book, aviation writer Roy Sloan concentrates on accidents to military aircraft in the main, giving a clear account of significant accidents such as the crash which led to the creation of the RAF's Mountain Rescue Organisation, and the remarkable escape of a Vulcan V-bomber's crew from their doomed aircraft — all of which make fascinating and compelling reading. Other titles by the author are *Early Aviation in North Wales* and *Wings of War over Gwynedd*.